Epworth Comm

General Ed

Ivor H. Jones

The Book of Ezekiel

The Book of
EZEKIEL

Charles R. Biggs

EPWORTH PRESS

Extracts from the Revised English Bible are © 1989
by the Delegates of the Oxford University Press and the
Syndics of the Cambridge University Press and are used
by permission

ISBN 0 7162 0505 X

First Published 1996
by Epworth Press
1 Central Buildings Westminster
London SW1H 9NR

Typeset by Regent Typesetting, London
Printed and bound in Great Britain by
Biddles Ltd, Guildford and King's Lynn

CONTENTS

Contents

GENERAL INTRODUCTION

The *Epworth Preachers's Commentaries* that Greville P. Lewis edited so successfully in the 1950s and 1960s having now served their turn, the Epworth Press has commissioned a team of distinguished academics who are also preachers and teachers to create a new series of commentaries that will serve the 1990s and beyond. We have seized the opportunity offered by the publication in 1989 of the Revised English Bible to use this very readable and scholarly version as the basis of our commentaries, and we are grateful to the Oxford and Cambridge University Presses for the requisite licence. Our authors will nevertheless be free to cite and discuss other translations wherever they think that these will illuminate the original text.

Just as the books that make up the Bible differ in their provenance and purpose, so our authors will necessarily differ in the structure and bearing of their commentaries. But they will all strive to get as close as possible to the intention of the original writers, expounding their texts in the light of the place, time, circumstances, and culture that gave them birth, and showing why each work was received by Jews and Christians into their respective Canons of Holy Scripture. They will seek to make full use of the dramatic advance in biblical scholarship world-wide but at the same time to explain technical terms in the language of the common reader, and to suggest ways in which Scripture can help towards the living of a Christian life today. They will endeavour to produce commentaries that can be used with confidence in ecumenical, multiracial, and multifaith situations, and not by scholars only but by preachers, teachers, students, church members, and anyone who wants to improve his or her understanding of the Bible.

Ivor H. Jones

PREFACE

The book of Ezekiel is not as well known as it deserves to be. It is an important part of the biblical tradition, dealing with a decisive period in the history of Israel when the people struggled to come to terms with what was happening to them in the context of their relationship with God. Ezekiel assisted in this process as he proclaimed God's words in ways that related to the experiences of the people, whether it be disobedience and judgement, punishment and repentance, or hope and renewal. That is, when the people struggled with a problem (for example, military defeat or exile), Ezekiel spoke about it in terms of their relationship with God and with their neighbours, pointed to God's understanding of things, called on them to take this seriously and summoned them to make their response to God who was with them in every experience.

When all this was brought together in the book of Ezekiel it gave a theological statement of Israel's experience from disobedience through judgement, punishment, repentance, forgiveness and renewal, which is of great value to us as we think about our relationship with God and the way in which we respond to God.

The aim of this book is to help people to understand what Ezekiel was saying to his people and the response he was expecting from them. It endeavours in a simple way to point to the profound truths that Ezekiel used to help people to discern the direction they should take as the people of God. It also points to a Christian appropriation of some of the major statements made by the book of Ezekiel.

I record my gratitude to the editors of the Epworth Commentaries for inviting me to contribute a volume to the series and especially for allowing me to work on a book in which I have a particular interest. It has been an interesting and rewarding task.

Thanks also to those who have persevered with me and encouraged me through the task, particularly my wife Margaret and my colleagues at Parkin-Wesley College. Grateful thanks also to Anna Catlin, Carol Cocks and Peter Whittington, colleagues in different parts of the theological endeavour, who read the text as it neared completion and offered helpful advice.

C.R.B.
February 1995

FOR FURTHER READING

Walther Zimmerli, *Ezekiel 1 and 2* (volume 1 translated by Ronald E. Clements; volume 2 translated by James D.Martin), Fortress Press 1979 and SCM Press 1983

This major modern commentary on Ezekiel works with the Hebrew Text but it may be read with comparative ease by those who have no Hebrew. A full translation is given and its discussion of exegesis and theology make it a valuable book.

Walther Eichrodt, *Ezekiel* (translated by Cosslett Quin), SCM Press 1970

John W. Wevers, *Ezekiel*, Eerdmans and Marshall, Morgan and Scott, 1982 (Based on the Revised Standard Version)

These commentaries also work with the Hebrew text. They give an English translation as well as the commentary and may be consulted with profit.

Keith W. Carley, *The Book of the Prophet Ezekiel*, Cambridge University Press 1974

A shorter commentary using the New English Bible translation.

Joseph Blenkinsopp, *Ezekiel*, John Knox Press 1990

Bruce Vawter and Leslie J. Hoppe, *Ezekiel*, Eerdmans and Handsel 1991

Two commentaries written for teaching and preaching which emphasise exposition and proclamation.

Keith W. Carley, *Ezekiel among the Prophets*, SCM Press 1975

A book which gives a general discussion on Ezekiel and his place in the prophetic trandition.

A simple atlas is a help in studying the Bible. A clear and informative atlas is:

Herbert G. May (ed.), *Oxford Bible Atlas*, Oxford University Press (revision and third edition John Day) 1984

INTRODUCTION

The book of Ezekiel is one of the three major books in the collection of prophetic material in the Hebrew scriptures. It contains material addressed to the people of Israel in the period immediately prior to the fall of Jerusalem to the Babylonians in 587 BCE, while they were in exile and after their return to their homeland.

The prophet and his time

Ezekiel – the person

Information about the prophet Ezekiel is available only from the book which bears his name. He is not mentioned elsewhere in the Hebrew scriptures, nor in contemporary literature. The purpose of the book is to record what Ezekiel said and did in proclaiming the word of God to his people at the crucial time of the fall of Jerusalem and Judah and the exile of the people to Babylon. Details on the life of Ezekiel are included in the book only where they would assist the reader to hear and accept what God had to say through the prophet. These details are few and certainly not enough to construct the life story of Ezekiel. They do however, establish that Ezekiel was an historical character who spoke to the people of Israel at an important time in their history.

Ezekiel was a priest who was taken into exile when the Babylonians captured Jerusalem in 597 BCE. In the fifth year of his exile, that is, in 593 BCE, he was called to be a prophet to the rebellious Israelites; and he continued as a prophet until 571 BCE. Ezekiel was married, but his wife died at the time of the fall of Jerusalem to the Babylonians. He mourned for her because she was 'the dearest thing' he had, but God forbade him to show his grief so that his suppressed mourning would be a sign to the people who were soon to suffer the loss of their beloved city (24.15–24).

Among the exiles Ezekiel was an important person. Three times elders of the people went to his house to sit with him and to seek his counsel (8.1; 14.1; 20.1) and on each occasion Ezekiel responded with an important statement of God's judgement on the disobedient people. These and other statements of judgement were addressed to people in Jerusalem and Judah which has led to the question, 'Did Ezekiel remain in Babylon, or did he return to Jerusalem for at least part of his life and prophesy there?' There is no evidence that he returned to Jerusalem. His addresses from exile were intended to warn the people of Judah and Jerusalem of the judgement that would certainly come to them if they continued in their disobedient ways and to remind the exiles that they had been judged and were suffering the appropriate punishment for their sins. His statements were also intended to show that the exile was a deserved punishment and a sign of God's continued care for the people; this was important for the exiles and part of the process toward their repentance and forgiveness by God. This understanding became significant after the fall of Jerusalem in 587 BCE as it enabled the people to see the need for repentance and gave them hope in God who cared for them and could forgive them.

The prophet's call is dominated by three things. First there was the overwhelming experience of the 'glory of God' (ch.1). Ezekiel knew that he had been in the presence of God and that it was God who called him to be a prophet. Second, he was commissioned to proclaim the word of God. This was symbolised by his being given a scroll to eat on which were written 'dirges and laments and words of woe', the theme for much of his preaching (2.9–3.3). Third, he had to speak to a rebellious house (2.4–11). In this Ezekiel's experience is similar to the call experiences of Isaiah and Jeremiah (Isa.6 and Jer.1) and, as with them, this experience continued with him through his activity as a prophet.

Historical background

Israel's prophets, and the books that resulted from their work, addressed specific situations in the life of the people of their time. For Ezekiel it was a time of great difficulty which caused the people and their leaders to question their understanding of God and their relationship with God.

Israel was a small nation situated on the major trade routes connecting the wealthy areas of Africa to the south-west and Asia to the north-east, which also were the routes taken by the great powers of those areas when they attempted to gain control of each other's territory. It was therefore in a position of strength and weakness.

Strength came from being in a strategic position to control the trade routes and so gain wealth by means of taxation and trade; weakness came from the almost constant threat from greater powers and their occupation of Israel's territory. Israel was frequently under the political control of other powers, with only brief periods when, due to a lack of any threatening outside power, it was free to pursue its own destiny. Assyria was the major power from 745 BCE till 627 BCE, Babylon from 605 BCE till 538 BCE and Persia from 538 BCE till 332 BCE. Egypt's power and influence in the area fluctuated during the period but, apart from its direct influence through occasional occupation of Israelite territory, it played an important role as a potential ally against the powers to the north-east.

In the time of Ezekiel, Babylon under Nebuchadrezzar was the dominating power. Nebuchadrezzar captured Jerusalem in 597 BCE, deposed King Jehoiachin, exiled him along with the leaders in the court, the army and the community and placed Zedekiah on the throne. Ezekiel was among those exiled, which suggests that at least some priests were taken into exile.

Zedekiah was a weak king who had to deal with the difficult problems of ruling a subject people and having to contend with groups which wanted Judah to follow a pro-Babylon, pro-Egyptian or independent nationalist policy. In 589 BCE, with support from Egypt, Judah openly rebelled against Babylon whose reaction was swift. Jerusalem was put under a long and terrible siege which, although it was interrupted briefly to deal with an attempted intervention by Egypt, eventually reduced Jerusalem to submission. Zedekiah attempted to escape but was caught, blinded and taken to Babylon. The city and temple were burned and the walls razed. A second deportation took place with a larger group taken into exile in Babylon where they were settled in their own communities, but far from their homeland. Those who remained in the land had a long struggle to survive in a devastated land now completely under foreign control as a province of Babylon. Israel's experience of monarchy was ended.

The fall and destruction of Jerusalem was a catastrophe for Israel for, in that experience, they lost those things which were the basis of their religion and their existence as a people. They lost the land, possession of which they traced to God's promises to Abraham (Gen.12.1; 15.18–19; 17.8) and to the oppressed people in Egypt (Exod.3.7–8,16–17; 13.5). It was God's gift to them and a sign of their relationship with God. They lost the temple which was more than the place where they worshipped their God, it was the sign of God's presence with them (I Kings 8.11,17–21,29; see also Ezek.8–11; 43.1–5). With the exile of Zedekiah and the execution of his sons they lost the monarchy which traced its line to David and the promise of God to him that there would always be a king of his line on the throne (II Sam.7.16). Jerusalem, the city won for them by David and which contained the temple, was lost. This was a great loss because they believed it was under God's protection and would be saved as it had been in the Assyrian attack during the reign of Hezekiah just over a century earlier (II Kings 19.21–34). Jeremiah's refutation of this belief shows that it still was current in the last days before the fall of the city (Jer.7.12–15).

The loss of these things struck at the heart of the religion of the people. Could they continue to believe they were God's people with such important things taken from them? If they were still God's people, how were they to understand God and their relationship with God? These basic questions provided the challenge to the exiles in Babylon to collect the traditions of the people, to study them in the light of this disastrous experience and to re-present them to the people as the essential basis of their continuing life with God. That they were successful is to be seen in the survival of the people, their strengthened hope in God who would save them and restore them, and the literature of the Hebrew scriptures which is available to us to-day.

The exile ended after the defeat of the Babylonians by the Persians under Cyrus in 539 BCE. Cyrus issued an edict in 538 BCE that the people were to return to their homeland, rebuild the temple in Jerusalem and re-establish their religion (II Chron.36.23). They returned to Jerusalem that same year but progress on rebuilding the temple was slow due to difficult economic times in Judah and to the tensions which arose between those who returned from Babylon with a refurbished religion and those who had remained in the land and claimed that they were the true inheritors of the land and faith of Israel (compare with Ezek.33.24–28). The temple was finally completed and dedicated in 516 BCE but the tensions between the groups continued to the time of Ezra and Nehemiah in the latter half of the following century.

The book: its structure and contents

Structure

The book has been compiled in five main sections; first, an account of the call of the prophet (chs.1–3); second, oracles of judgement against Jerusalem and Judah, which are set in the period before the fall of Jerusalem (chs.4–24); third, oracles against foreign nations (chs.25–32); fourth, oracles of hope for those in exile (chs.33–39); fifth, a vision of the renewed temple, regulations for its cult and the distribution of the tribes of Israel in the land on their return and renewal after the exile (chs.40–48).

The structure of the book reflects the experience of the people as it was seen in terms of their relationship with God. They were disobedient, which brought God's judgement on them and their punishment in exile, but they were not cast off by God; rather, the exile became an opportunity for them to repent. God forgave them, restored them to their homeland and provided the means for their continued relationship with God through a rebuilt temple set in the midst of their life as a people.

Contents

The material in the book is of complex character. There are oracles from Ezekiel proclaiming judgement, punishment, repentance and hope. These oracles have been expanded and adapted to meet the needs of the people at later times and to help them to see that not only were they rightly judged by God, but the judgement would lead to forgiveness and restoration if they would repent. This may have been done by the prophet himself and reflect his change from a prophet of judgement and doom before the exile to a prophet of hope and renewal when Jerusalem fell in 587 BCE and the major exile took place. At least some adaptation of the oracles appears to have been the work of others who wrote at a later time, either in co-operation with Ezekiel or independently. The construction of the material points to a group of people having worked on the oracles for the benefit of the exiles. Similarities with the literature of Deuteronomy, the Deuteronomic History (Joshua-II Kings) and the Holiness Code (Lev.17–26) show that the influences on the group were complex. They also show that different theological emphases came together to meet the needs of the exiles as they sought to know what God had to say to them in that new situation.

Oracles of judgement follow charges that the people had been unfaithful through involvement in other cults and/or alliances with foreign powers. The charges are vividly spelled out in chs. 16 and 23 where the prophet compared Jerusalem with an unfaithful woman who was involved in harlotry and adultery. As an adulteress would be judged and punished, so would Jerusalem be judged and punished. In bringing the charge in this way Ezekiel drew on and developed the work of Hosea and Jeremiah, each of whom saw Israel's unfaithfulness as the betrayal of the relationship with God and the cause of its destruction. Ezekiel did not simply borrow from his predecessors, he took up their statements of the word of God proclaimed for earlier times and represented them so that they became God's word for the situation of the people of his time.

In ch.20 the charge is presented in the form of a survey of Israel's history. It shows how Israel was under judgement at a number of points in its history, but, for the sake of God's name, no action was taken until God swore to send them into exile because they were disobedient, for they did not conform to God's statutes or observe God's laws, but they desecrated God's sabbaths.

The judgement proclaimed by the prophet was usually in terms of a siege of Jerusalem and a military catastrophe. The day of judgement would be a terrible day with destruction coming through the sword, famine and pestilence. Ezekiel had no doubt Jerusalem would be destroyed. It had become like a charred piece of useless vine wood so it would be given up to the fire (ch.15).

The offer of hope for those who had experienced judgement and were suffering punishment in exile is a prominent feature in the book. In the major section on hope (chs.33–37) Ezekiel assured the exiles that God would act to restore and renew them as they took the opportunity God gave them to repent. God would give the repentant people a new spirit and a new heart to enable them to be obedient when they returned to their homeland (11.19–20; 36.26–28).

Statements of hope have been added to oracles of judgement in earlier chapters of the book. For example, in ch.16 the people are charged, judged and punishment pronounced in vv.1–58; then it is said that God would remember the covenant made at the beginning of Israel's history and establish an everlasting covenant with them (vv.59–63). Similarly, to the words of judgement which came through the review of Israel's history in ch.20.1–31 was added a promise that the exiles would return and their return would be like the exodus from Egypt (vv.32–44). Brief hopeful comments occur among other judgement oracles; for example, the prophet was commanded to shave the hair from his body and destroy it in three ways to symbolise the method of destruction for the people of Jerusalem (5.1–2). To this was added a further command to keep a small portion of one part to show that not all the people would be destroyed (vv.3–4). That is, there was hope for some whom God would save, presumably the exiles.

In all the hope passages the emphasis is on God's action to save and renew the people. God would establish the covenant with them (16.60,62), search for them and seek them out (34.11–16) and bring them from the lands where they had been scattered (20.34–42).

The final section of the book, in the form of a vision, gives plans for the temple and the allocation of land for the tribes of Israel in the restored homeland. The importance of the temple for the restored and renewed people is stressed in the plans for the complex of buildings and the altar, and in the regulations for priestly service and provision for the temple cult (40–46). The allocation of the land with the temple in the centre of the tribal areas emphasises the same point (47.13–48.35). Entry of the 'glory of God' into the temple would be the assurance that God's presence was among the people (43.1–5) and the sign that the relationship between God and Israel had been renewed. The temple in the midst of the people would play a vital part in maintaining that relationship.

Significant in the structure of the book and the presentation of its message are the accounts of four visions in which God's dealing with the people was made known to the prophet. Three of the visions involved experiences of the 'glory of God', the vision of the 'glory of God' and the call of the prophet (1.1–3.15), the departure of the 'glory of God' from the temple (8–11) and the plans for the temple and the return of the 'glory of God' to it (40.1–43.12). The accounts of these three visions have undergone some revision to ensure that the connections between them are apparent to the reader. The major points they make are that:

1. Ezekiel had been in the presence of God. He was called and authenticated as a true prophet to the people of God.

2. God would reject the people and end the relationship by withdrawing the 'glory of God' from the temple.

3. God would provide for the maintenance of the renewed relationship with a new temple and the return of the 'glory of God' to it.

The fourth vision, that of the dry bones reassembled and restored to life (37.1–14), is different from the other three in that the 'glory of God' does not have a part in it. It comes between the two visions concerning the temple to bring the message of hope that God would revive and restore the people devastated by God's rejection and their exile far from their homeland. As in the visions concerning the temple, the prophet experienced the hand of God upon him and the spirit of God transporting him to the place of the vision.

The visions represent the major points of the book; that is, the people were disobedient, they would be judged and punished in exile, they would be restored by the action of God, God would renew the relationship and provide the means for it to continue. They form major points of emphasis in the structure of the book.

Sexual language, imagery and metaphor

Many people, particularly women, have difficulty with the sexual language, imagery and metaphors used by Ezekiel to convey his message to the people. This is especially so in chs.16 and 23 where the prophet drew on the work of his predecessors and used a metaphor of female sexual infidelity to describe Israel's and Judah's betrayal of their relationship with God.

The metaphor is seen to reflect a patriarchal society in which women were subservient to men. For example, in matters of sex and marriage, men had much more freedom than women and sexual offences committed by a woman were considered to be committed against the man who was responsible for her; that is, her husband or father. In addition, the way in which the metaphor is used, particularly Ezekiel's graphic description and his details of offences and punishments, has been seen as derogatory to all women in that it suggests that women are not only unfaithful but also aggressively immoral in their sexual activity. As such, the material in Ezekiel 16 and 23 has been described by some writers as pornography which, like all pornography, is used as a means of maintaining the subservient role of women in society.

It has been noted also by some writers that the metaphor casts God in the role of the faithful husband and Israel/Judah as the unfaithful woman, further emphasising the superior position of the male, the basis of the patriarchal system. At a time when Western society is becoming increasingly aware of discrimination against women and striving to deal with it, the use of this metaphor in proclamation of the word of God is being seriously questioned.

There is no doubt that we need to deal with sexual discrimination in our society, but we also need to deal with the text before us. When faced with Ezekiel 16 and 23, our revulsion at the metaphor, its background and its details, may be an important part of the impact the text has on us.

There are two things to be noted. First, the characterisation of the women in such a negative way as unfaithful wives involved in adultery and harlotry is not the only way in which women and their roles are depicted in the Bible. There are significant positive references which help us to understand the nature of God and our relationship with God. For example; in marriage, provision was made for the role of each partner – the husband was obliged to provide for his wife and protect her (Exod.21.10–11) and the wife was required to obey her husband and refrain from sexual relations with other men (Num.5.11–15,29–30; 30.1–16). But that does not describe the relationship; there was also love. For example, Isaac loved his wife Rebecca (Gen.24.67), Elkanah loved Hannah (1 Sam.1.5) and, when Ezekiel's wife died God said, 'I am taking from you … the dearest thing you have' (Ezek.24.16). God's description of the loss of the temple, which was as devastating to the people as was the loss of his wife to Ezekiel, is in terms of the loss of a beloved wife; 'the delight of their eyes, their heart's desire' (v.25). The description of the relationship between God and Israel in terms of marriage draws on the characteristics of faithfulness and love.

The loving care, nurture and compassion of God are described in terms of these qualities as seen in women and particularly mothers; for example, 'As a mother comforts her son so shall I myself comfort you;' (Isa.66.13; see also 42.14). The love of God is compared to the love of a mother for her child because that love is the most reliable and constant love that is known (Isa.49.15; also Isa.46.3–4). We also have to recognise the devotion of parents (father *and* mother) which the psalmist draws on in the expression of God's faithfulness to Israel; 'Though my father and my mother forsake me, the Lord will take me into his care' (Ps.27.10).

Second, Ezekiel, like his predecessors Hosea and Jeremiah, appears to have made great efforts to shock the people by the language and metaphors he used. His description of God's departure from the temple and the destruction of the people of Jerusalem were intended to shock them into recognising how great were the consequences of their actions and their forsaking of God (chs.9–10). Similarly, his review of the history of Israel raised and emphasised points in that history to shock the people into acknowledging their record of faithlessness which continued in exile in Babylon (ch.20).

The sexual language, images and metaphors used by the prophet have the same purpose and effect. There is no suggestion that what Ezekiel presents as the activity of the women in chs.16 and 23 was the norm for women in Judah and Israel. Rather, Ezekiel chose a metaphor which was so different from the way women generally acted that it would shock and outrage the hearers and, hopefully, cause them to realise the enormity of their situation. To emphasise the point further, the people addressed by the prophet were in the main the men of Judah who controlled the political and religious life of the nation. They were being accused of actions which were horrible and loathsome. Surely they would recognise their position and change their ways.

Chapters 16 and 23 remain before us. For some people the metaphor used is so repulsive that they will have to leave the passages to one side. For others, that same repulsiveness may sharpen the point the prophet made and turn them to a new understanding and relationship with God.

Use of Israel's traditions

A number of traditions important to the life of Israel have formed the basis of the book of Ezekiel. Traditions of earlier prophets, particularly those of Hosea and Jeremiah, have been used in chs.16 and 23 (see above). The 'Day of the Lord' (13.5; 30.1–9; 'the day', 7.7–19) as a day of woe and destruction shares similar thoughts with Amos (5.18–20; 8.3,9–10), Isaiah (2.12,20; 3.18; 13.6–16) and Zephaniah (1.14–18).

Israel as a vine is a strong tradition found in the wilderness account (Num.13) and in the prophets Hosea, Isaiah and Jeremiah (Hos.10; Isa.5; Jer.2). In Ezekiel's hands the tradition of Israel as a fruitful vine was reduced to an absurdity as he ignored the fruit of the vine to deal with its useless wood and thus show how worthless Jerusalem had become in the eyes of God (ch.15). This use of the vine tradition is a good example of Ezekiel's creativity in the use of material available to him. He used the traditions of his people, popular stories (the foundling, 16.1–14, notorious sisters, 23.1–4) and sayings of the people (sour grapes, 18.2, inheriting the land, 33.24) to help the people to know the state of their relationship with God and the calamity that was to befall them.

In ch.20 the exodus and wilderness traditions were drawn on to

show that Israel was disobedient in Egypt; that is, from the beginning of its relationship with God. In the latter part of ch.20 the same
traditions are used to proclaim the promise of God's intention to
return the people to their homeland. The return would be like a
second exodus and testing in the wilderness (vv.34–38).

The law formed the basis for the judgement pronounced by the
prophet. The form of the law tradition found in the Holiness Code
(Lev.17–26) is particularly close to Ezekiel (see for example
Ezek.34.23–31 and Lev.26.4–13). In addition, the prophet appears to
have been aware of lists of laws which may have been used in the
cult to determine the righteousness of a person (see for example
ch.18).

The purpose of the book

The purpose of the book of Ezekiel was to help the people of Israel to
understand the nature of their relationship with God and to show
them how, when the relationship had been broken, it might be
renewed and then maintained. Ezekiel proclaims that obedience was
the response God required from the people and when that was not
forthcoming the relationship would be ended and the people punished. However, God was faithful even to the faithless people, so if
the people would repent, God would forgive them, restore the relationship and provide them with a new way of life.

The book makes it plain that the renewal of the people would be
the work of God. God would give them a new heart and a new spirit
so that they could respond with obedience to God, return them to
their homeland, restore the devastated land and give them a new
temple set in the midst of their tribes and at the centre of their life.
The 'glory of God' in the temple would be the assurance that they
were God's people who made response to God by their service in the
temple and by their observance of the law.The book of Ezekiel also
stresses that God's dealing with Israel made God known to Israel
and to the nations and that it was God's intention to do this. The
'recognition formula', 'that you (they) may know that I am the Lord',
which occurs many times in Ezekiel, shows this.

The phrase, 'I am the Lord' (or 'I am Yahweh'), is in the form of a
self-introduction in which a person is revealed by making known his
or her name. It is used in this way in the preamble to the Decalogue
where God's opening words are, 'I am the Lord (Yahweh) your
God', followed by reference to God's actions in bringing the people
out of Egypt and then by the commandments (Ex.20.2). God is

revealed in making known his name and the immediate impact of
the being of God on the people of Israel is acknowledged in the
actions leading up to the conclusion of the covenant. Whenever it is
used subsequently, the self-introduction formula points to the com-
munication of God's self as revealed in the past and as it is known
anew in the further actions of God.

The first part of the formula, 'that you may know', points to know-
ing in the sense of recognising who God is, with the claim which the
knowledge makes, that there be a response to 'the Lord' who has
been encountered in God's acts in history. In Ezekiel the 'recognition
formula' is connected with accounts of God's actions towards Israel
and the nations. It is usually a conclusion to statements of judgement, punishment, forgiveness, renewal and restoration and shows
that what God did was directed toward having Israel and the nations
acknowledge God as Lord. Ezekiel proclaimed that, in God's actions,
God was seeking relationship with Israel and the nations, a relationship characterised by the knowledge that God is the Lord; that is,
God over all.

COMMENTARY

The call of Ezekiel
1.1–3.27

The record of the call of the prophet Ezekiel begins with an introduction which also serves to introduce the book of Ezekiel (vv.1–3). This is followed by a vision of the 'glory of the Lord' (vv.4–28a;3.12–15), and the call and commissioning of the prophet (1.28b–3.11).

Introduction and superscription
1.1–3

The introduction is in three parts. Verse 1 gives the date and place where the prophet received the *visions of God* which follow in vv.4–28. The date, although stated as the *thirtieth year*, cannot be identified with any precision because it lacks a point of reference. The further statement that the prophet was among the *exiles by the river Kebar* in Babylon puts it sometime after 597 BCE, but it does not offer any further help.

Various suggestions have been made to identify the point of reference. One is that it was thirty years after the discovery of the 'book of the law' in the temple in 621 BCE (II Kings 22–23), which approximates the date given in v.2; that is, 593 BCE. This is not easily accepted because of all the dates in the book, it would be the only one that did not use the first exile of the people by Nebuchadrezzar in 597 BCE as the point of reference.

Another possibility is that it refers to the prophet's age at the time of the vision and call. Ezekiel is identified as a priest in v.3. Thirty was the age of entry into the priesthood (Num.4.3,30). At the age when this would normally happen Ezekiel was in Babylon, away from the temple in Jerusalem, and unable to take up priestly tasks. At that important age he may have been called to be a prophet to his exiled and suffering people. This is possible. There is no direct supporting evidence, but neither is there anything to deny it.

1.2. gives another date for what follows, relating it to the first deportation of the people to Babylon. It is in accord with the other dates given in the book, except that in 1.1, which puts the vision and the call in the year 593/2 BCE. The two dates in ch.1 belong to the development processes of the book. The date in 1.2 which (like all others except 1.1) relates to the exile of 597 BCE, is part of the present structure of the book. The *thirtieth year* is a piece of further information given to assist people to accept the importance and authority of the book.

1.3 gives a standard form of heading which is found at the beginning of other prophetic books; for example, Hosea, Joel, Haggai, and Zechariah. This establishes what follows as the word of God to Israel.

A vision of the glory of the Lord
   1.4–28a

The vision narrative has been elaborated by followers of the prophet who have contributed to the extremely vivid nature of the symbolism.

1.4 The narrative begins with the description of a storm (v.4). It appears that the prophet's experience of this natural event became the occasion for the vision from which the present account grew. The association of God's 'appearance' by way of a storm with strong winds, thunder and lightning is found in other places in the Old Testament; for example, on Mount Sinai (Exod.19.16), in answer to a cry for help (Ps.18.7–14 [Hebrew Text 8–15]), to Job who heard God out of a whirlwind (Job 40.6), and for Elijah who expected God to appear in a storm (I Kings.19.11). The storm was an established vehicle for a vision of God.

1.5–14 The account which follows describes what Ezekiel saw in the storm. The flashing fire and light was what one might see when looking into the coals of a fire (v.14). He saw likenesses of creatures with human bodies and the features of animals and birds. They had four faces, one human, two animal, and one of a bird. Such awe-inspiring creatures were known in other ancient religions in relation to their gods and temples. They lend a sense of wonder and mystery to the description of the 'vision of God'.

1.15–21   introduce a new feature to the description of the vision. Beside each of the creatures the prophet saw a complex wheel structure, *a wheel within a wheel*, which may mean that each wheel consisted of two wheels mounted concentrically, or at right angles to one another. The creatures and the wheels moved together, both horizontally and vertically.

This description may be a reference to God as a king who rides in a royal chariot such as those used by the kings of Israel and Judah (I Kings 22.35; II Kings 9.27; 9.16). Elsewhere God is said to ride in a chariot of victory (Hab.3.8) and in chariots 'like the storm wind' (Isa.66.15). The passage further emphasises the splendour and majesty of God and connects with statements about circling wheels and cherubim in chs.10 and 11, which deal with the departure of the 'glory of the Lord' from the temple and the city of Jerusalem.

1.22–28a Here the purpose of the living creatures becomes apparent; they carried a platform (vault) above their heads on which stood a throne of sapphire. On the throne was a being whom the prophet could only describe in terms of wonder and awe – *human likeness, brass glowing like fire in a furnace, looked like fire* and *radiance encircled him* (vv.26–27). All of these terms avoid a description of the being. They are traditional expressions which convey the reality of the presence of God and the splendour and glory known in God's presence.

The climax of the vision was in the prophet's recognition of what he saw; *it was like the appearance of the glory of the Lord* (v.28a). *The glory of the Lord* is a technical term for the presence of God among the people of Israel, and the sign of its presence was a 'cloud' (Exod.40.35). It was said to dwell in the temple in Jerusalem (I Kings 8.10–11), and was the assurance that God was among the people.

THE VISION – GOD WITH THE PEOPLE

An important point made in the presentation of the vision is that the 'glory of the Lord' appeared to Ezekiel in Babylon. The prophet was far from the temple in Jerusalem where the 'glory' was believed to be and, indeed, far from the land of the people of God. Because of this, when the vision was recalled, it gave to the people in exile the message that they were not far from God, rather, God was with them. It was therefore a note of hope for those who suffered the judgement and the punishment of God (see also on 11.16 below).

A further point of importance is that the prophet saw God as one who was not tied to the geographical region of the land of Israel. Rather, God was seen to be beyond such limitations, one who came to an Israelite prophet in Babylon and commanded him to speak to his fellow exiles in Babylon. The vision presents the understanding of the effective presence of God which is to be seen also in what follows in the call to Ezekiel in chs. 2.1–3.15. In a foreign land God appeared to Ezekiel, called him to be a prophet and sent him to speak in God's name to the exiles in Babylon.

This same effective presence of God is to be seen in other places in the book of Ezekiel, such as in God's dealing with Israel in Egypt (20.5–7), the action in bringing them out of Egypt (20.8–9) and leading them through the wilderness (20.11–17). The prophecies against foreign nations (chs. 25–32) proclaim God's will and effectiveness in determining the course of the history of the nations. All of these references to God and the nations assured the people of Israel that their God was with them wherever they might go, indeed, in Ezekiel's presentation, wherever God might lead them or drive them.

God's unrestricted presence in the world is foundational to the Christian faith. We affirm the importance of certain places where God may be sought with an assurance borne out by the experience of people through the ages, but we also know that wherever we go God is there and may be sought by us. The key to this is in the understanding that God is God of the universe, not just of parts of it and that God offers relationship with people, relationship that is not geographically determined. So the Christian can say with conviction the words of Psalm 139 as it reminds us that there is no place we may go that God is not already there. The traditions of the church and the experiences of its people declare it.

There is a practical feature to this point. Mobility is a feature of modern life. People move to other towns, cities, regions or countries in search of work, career or education. In doing this they leave behind not only family, friends and objects, but also that which belongs to their spiritual being. People who leave an area where they have a strong attachment to a congregation may find it hard to form a link with the church in their new environment. The physical things that embodied the church in their former place may not be present in the same way in the new locality and they may appear to have lost their faith with the transfer. Our task is to help people to develop their spiritual lives in such a way that they appreciate the support of their `home ties' but are sufficiently independent of them to maintain faith when these ties have to been broken. There is also a need for church communities to assist newcomers to recognise God's presence in the community itself and in the place where it celebrates God's presence.

The call and commission
1.28b–3.15

Ezekiel's response to this overwhelming experience of the 'glory of God' was to fall on his face in awe at the presence of God. A similar experience is recorded in the account of the 'call' of the prophet Isaiah. Isaiah's response to the presence of God in the temple was to acknowledge that he had unclean lips and that he dwelt among a people of unclean lips (Isa.6.5). The sense of awe experienced by the prophets immobilised them until God acted to enable each one to respond to the call. Isaiah's lips were cleansed (v.7), and a spirit stood Ezekiel on his feet (2.2).

2.3–5   The call to Ezekiel then came to him in the form of a commissioning to go to the rebellious Israelites with the *words of the Lord God* (v.4). That is, Ezekiel was sent as a messenger to the people. The three parts of the commissioning show this. God said *'I am sending you ... you are to say ... they will know'* (vv.3–5). By the words of this man the people would hear God's word to them, and when he used the formula *these are the words of the Lord God*, they would recognise that he was a prophet. (Compare the story of Na'aman in II Kings 5, especially vv.8 and 15.)

2.6–7   This recognition did not guarantee the people of Israel would accept what the prophet had to say (v.7). It was more likely they would resist and reject the prophet and his words. Their rebellious looks and words would cause him to fear, but at God's command he had to speak, whether they listened or not. This was the task of a messenger. Similar words of strength and encouragement were given to Jeremiah (Jer.1.7–8) and Isaiah was warned that the people to whom he was sent would not receive what he had to say (Isa.6.9–10).

2.8–3.2   The role of the messenger as a person who spoke the words

7

of the one who sent him is further emphasised in the command to eat the scroll God gave to Ezekiel. Written on the scroll was God's message of *dirges and laments and words of woe* (2.9). This was the message given by God and which Ezekiel, the faithful messenger, had to deliver to Israel. The command to eat the scroll ensured that the message was part of the very being of Ezekiel and would continue with him throughout his ministry (v.3).

The call of Ezekiel is similar to the call of Jeremiah. After the initial statement of call to Jeremiah and his objection that he was too young to be a prophet, God touched his mouth and said 'I have put my words in your mouth' (Jer. 1.9; see also Deut.18.18, 'I (God) will put my words in his (the prophet's) mouth'). Ezekiel's account is more dramatic in its movement and the build up of the passage, but both narratives emphasise that the prophet spoke the word of God and therefore the people should have listened to him. The call narrative not only authenticates the spoken words of the prophet, it also gives authority to the words of the book that follow.

Reference to a prophet eating the words of God is also found in Jer.15.16. Jeremiah lamented the treatment he received from those to whom he took the words God gave him to speak (Jer.15.15–18), but within this complaint he also recalled that he ate the words and they 'became a joy and delight' in his heart (v.16).

The next part of the call narrative specifies the people to whom the message of God was to be delivered. Ezekiel was sent to the *Israelites*, literally 'the house of Israel'; that is, to his own people. Ezekiel used the term 'Israel' for the people of God, the people with whom God had a covenant relationship and at the time of his call that referred to the people in exile (see vv.10–11). The message which the book gives is one of indictment, judgement, and punishment to God's disobedient people. The purpose was to encourage the people to repent in order that they might be forgiven and have their relationship with God restored. This applied particularly to the exiles who had been judged and were suffering the just punishment for their disobedience.

3.4–9   The difficulty the prophet would have in gaining a hearing from the rebellious people, referred to in 2.6–8, is addressed again here. As an 'Israelite', Ezekiel spoke the same language as the people so there would not be any difficulty for the people in understanding what he was saying (vv.5–6). The problem was that they would refuse to listen to him. So God warned Ezekiel (v.7), as Isaiah before him had been warned (Isa.6.9–10), that his words would not be heeded. God provided for such discouragement by making the prophet as strong as the people and *harder than* brass, emery (or *adamant*) and *flint* (vv.8–9). A similar assurance was given to Jeremiah (1.18).

3.10–11 concludes the commission by summarising what the prophet was to do. He had to *listen, take to heart, go* to his *fellow-countrymen in exile* and say *the words of the Lord God*. This makes it clear that Ezekiel's words were addressed to the exiles, even though they at times referred to Judah and Jerusalem and what was happening there.

3.12–15   The call and vision narrative is completed with a reference back to the beginning in ch.1. Having received his call, the prophet was transported by *a spirit* to the place where the exiles were settled, *by the river Kebar* (1.1,3; 3.15), and there he was in *a state of consternation* for seven days. The whole experience remained in the prophet's memory throughout his ministry and the account of it was placed in a prominent place at the beginning of the book which presented his words and experiences. Similarly, Isaiah and Jeremiah had dramatic call experiences which have been preserved for us (Isa.6; Jer.1).

The prophet as a warning
   3.16–21

A further interpretation of the task of the prophet is given in vv.16b–21 (v.16a makes the connection with what has gone before). The prophet is seen as a watchman with the task of warning the people that they should turn from their *wicked ways*. The awesome task of a prophet is portrayed in these verses. He would be held responsible for the fate of those he did not warn that God's judgement was about to fall on them (see also ch.33.1–9).

   There is also a connection with the prophetic theme found in the books of Kings that, throughout the history of the monarchy, God spoke through prophets to warn Israel of the consequences of disobedience and apostasy (see, for example, II Kings 17.13). Ezekiel is portrayed as a prophet in that line and one whose words of warning were fulfilled.

Constrained to speak at God's direction

3.22–27

In these verses it is made clear that the prophet was to speak only at God's direction. He was sent out into *the plain* where God spoke to him and directed him to shut himself in his house, be *bound with ropes*, and have his tongue stick to his mouth. He would thus be unable to speak to *that rebellious people* except when God had something to say to them. Then Ezekiel would receive back the power of speech, and say, *This is what the Lord God said* (v.27).

This passage contains close similarities to other parts of the book. 3.22–24a connects the passage with the vision/call narrative as it refers to 'the Lord's hand upon me' (1.3), the 'glory of the Lord' (1.28), by the river Kebar (1.1,3), and 'set me on my feet' (2.2). The second half of v.27, with reference to 'rebels' and listening, takes up words from 2.5b and 3.11. A strong case is thus made for seeing the passage as part of the call narrative (1.1–3.16), or an interpretation of it.

The binding of the prophet is similar to the symbolic action of ch.4.4–8 (especially v.8). His inability to speak (v.26) was also part of the prophet's experience at the time of the fall of Jerusalem (24.15–27; 33.21–22). Verses 22–27 emphasise that the prophet was called to speak the word of God to the rebellious people as God directed him. It thus forms a bridge between the vision/call narrative and the condemnation of the people which follows in chs.4–24.[The REB suggests by the heading at v.22 that vv.22–27 belong with chs.4 and 5. The lack of an introductory statement at the beginning of ch.4 suggests that we are intended to see v.22a as the introduction to a new section – Judgement on Jerusalem and the Land (chs. 3.22–7.27).]

THE CALL OF GOD

The call of God to the prophet Ezekiel, so graphically recalled in these first three chapters, is to be seen within the context of the relationship established when God called Israel to be the people of God ('out of Egypt I called my son' Hos. 11.1). Individuals, such as Ezekiel, were called to play their part in the relationship by summoning the people to respond to God with obedience and service, and repentance when they had been disobedient.

The call of Ezekiel establishes three essentials in relation to the prophet and the book. First, the prophet had experienced the closeness of God's presence and that experience lived with him for the whole of his prophetic activity. He knew from experience that God had called him and had given him the words, the strength and courage to proclaim God's message to the disobedient people.

Second, as a result of the call from God, Ezekiel was enlisted into a particular service of God. That is, his function from that time on was related to the work of a prophet, speaking and acting in the name of God. He was a messenger, making known what it was God wanted the people of Israel to know and exhorting the people to respond to God.

Third, the establishment of Ezekiel as a prophet in this call narrative gives authority to the words which follow in the book as words from God. Thus the call brings ongoing acknowledgment to the prophet and to his words.

Accounts of God's call to people to take particular directions in life or undertake specific tasks are found in many places in the Bible and the history of the church. For example, Abraham was called to leave his own country to travel to another country to found a new nation through whom the peoples of the earth would be blessed (Gen.12.1–3); Moses was called to lead his people out of slavery in Egypt (Ex.3; 6.1–13); Isaiah (Isa.6), Jeremiah (Jer.1) Ezekiel (Ezek.2–3) and Amos (Amos 7) were called to be prophets of God to Israel. The previous life experience of these people was varied. Moses was working as a shepherd when he was called, Amos appears to have been from the country and worked as a 'herdsman and fig-grower', Isaiah was associated with the royal court, while Ezekiel was a priest and Jeremiah came from a priestly family.

The New Testament also has examples of people called to be God's messengers, most notably the disciples Simon (Peter) and Andrew, who were bidden to leave their fishing, follow Jesus and be 'fishers of men' (Mark 1.16–18), James and John, also fishermen (Mark 1.19–20), Levi, the tax collector (Luke 5.27–28) and Philip and Nathanael (John 1.43–51.; see also Matth. 4.18–22). Saul, who became Paul, also knew himself to be called by God as he records in the letter to the Romans; 'called by God to be an apostle and set apart for the service of his gospel' (Rom.1.1; 1 Cor.1.1).

When we examine these examples we see that the call of God was a life-changing event for these people, characterised by a sense of the overwhelming presence of God which overcame their initial reluctance and feeling of inadequacy and affected every part of their lives. They thus became people who were able to fulfil the commission of God to them, always aware of their need of God's continuing presence, guidance and power.

The church throughout its history has had men and women similarly called who have led, guided, inspired and blessed its people and the people of the world. There have been those like Thomas à Kempis and Julian of Norwich who provided for many a way to deepened spiritual awareness and perception, Francis of Assisi who explored simplicity of life and harmony with God's creation, Luther, Calvin and other reformers who challenged the church and radically changed its direction, the Wesleys who reasserted the need to proclaim the gospel to all people, Martin Luther King and Desmond Tutu who have struggled against racism in the church and in the world community and Mother Teresa whose very being among the poorest, most neglected and forsaken people has given hope and dignity to them and displayed the compassion of the committed follower of Jesus Christ.

All of these people have responded to the call of God. They are or were aware of God's continuing presence with them, which enabled them to do what they believed God commissioned them to do. In their response to God they were a blessing to people as they shared their own deep awareness of God and their concern for people.

These are examples of the faithful who have responded to the call of God and there have been countless others who have responded in faith and brought about blessing and change in their own more limited spheres of life, who, because of God's call to them, exhibit an ongoing awareness of God and a concern for others which brings people into the presence of God.

The circumstances in which God may call a person vary greatly but the response God seeks is constant; acknowledgment of God's blessing and acceptance of the life and work to which God has called the person. So the called may be found in any and every walk of life, being God's person in all that life brings to them.

Judgement on Jerusalem and Judah
4–24

The coming destruction of Jerusalem
4–5

A number of Ezekiel's prophetic actions and their interpretations are presented in chapters 4 and 5. The purpose is to portray the inevitability of God's judgement on Jerusalem and to show why the city had to be destroyed and its people exiled.

PROPHETIC ACTIONS

Dramatic actions were performed by the prophets of Israel to give greater impact to the message they had to proclaim in the name of God. For example, Isaiah walked naked and barefoot to tell of the captivity and exile which would befall a disobedient people (Isa.20), Jeremiah broke an earthenware jar to show how Jerusalem and its people would be smashed by God (Jer.19); and here we have Ezekiel with his drawing on a tile, baking with mixed grain, shaving with a sword (chs.4 and 5), and preparing for exile (ch.12). When the action was performed before the people, it brought into their consciousness with particular force the reality of what it symbolized.

Certain features may be discerned in these actions which help in identifying them as prophetic. First, they were performed by people who acknowledged a particularly close relationship with God, a relationship from which came both the direction to declare God's word to the people and the strength to do so. Declaring God's word in some instances involved actions which dramatically portrayed for the people what God had to say to them. What the prophet did was a sign to the people of what was to come, a particularly potent sign, for, when the action had taken place, its fulfilment was inevitable.

Second, the prophetic action was undertaken usually at the command of God, although this may not be stated in the account of the action. Third, a prophetic action took place once only as it related to

13

a particular time in the people's relationship with God. However, the account of the action enabled it to have an ongoing effect in the life of the people as the prophetic traditions were recalled and applied to new situations in the relationship. Fourth, an oracle or some explanation of the action was usually given to point out the meaning of the action and to relate it to the circumstances in which it was enacted.

Prophetic actions played an important role in the work of the prophets. They were, at times, somewhat bizarre, but that contributed to the potency with which the prophet's message was delivered to the disobedient people. (For a discussion on prophetic actions see W.D.Stacey, *Prophetic Drama in the Old Testament*, Epworth Press, London, 1990.)

Portraying a siege

4.1–3

There are two instructions to the prophet in these verses, both related to the siege of a city. First, the prophet was told to draw a city on a tile, that is, a clay tile which had not been baked to harden it. The assumption is that the city was Jerusalem, as the addition, the city of Jerusalem, makes plain (v.1). Around this representation of the city the prophet had to portray the implements of a siege (v.2). This was a prophetic action used by Ezekiel to show what God had in store for the city and which, by its performance, would bring about God's action. That is, the prophet had to tell of the consequences of the actions of God's rebellious people, and enact the judgement of God against them. Such a prophetic act would have a strong effect on the people as it presented visibly what the prophet had to say, so raising within them fear of what was to happen and convincing them that what the prophet enacted would take place.

The second instruction, to put an iron plate between himself and the city, expressed God's determination to judge the city (v.3a). Nothing could break through the iron barrier which separated the prophet from the city. The city was rejected. The prophet's role as the proclaimer of judgement was affirmed in this addition to vv.1–2. The final comment stressed the importance of Ezekiel's action; it would be a sign to Israel, as would the prophet himself as he performed this and other dramatic actions at the command of God.

Bearing punishment

4.4–8

In these verses there is a further instruction to the prophet. He was to lie on his left side 390 days (v.4) and on his right side 40 days (v.6). Each day was to signify a year of punishment to be endured by Israel and Judah. It also stated that the prophet was to be seen as the bearer of the punishment of the people (v.5), a concept which appears to have arisen in the latter part of the exilic period, and may be compared to the Suffering Servant of Isaiah (Isa.52.13–53.12). The addition of vv.7–8 directly relates the punishment to the judgement of vv.1–2.

Forty years was not the exact period of Judah's punishment in exile (587 to 538 BCE), but forty is a traditional figure that indicates a period of time in which significant things occurred in Israel's life with God; for example, forty years in the wilderness (Num.14.33–35; 32.13), a period for one generation to die out and be replaced by another and the forty days and nights of the great flood (Gen.7.4–7; 8.6). The term is used in a similar way in this text to indicate that the exile was a time of great significance for Judah (Israel).

The period of punishment for Israel, 390 years, presents us with a much greater problem. If the end of that punishment was the end of the exile, that is, 538 BCE, its commencement would have been the division of Israel into two kingdoms (Israel and Judah) in approximately 920 BCE. This would assume that the period of separation of the northern kingdom from Judah was to be understood as exile for the people of that kingdom. It would then be a theological statement on the relationship of the northern kingdom to God, which is portrayed in I and II Kings as one of consistent disobedience in that the kings 'followed in Jeroboam's footsteps, repeating the sin which Jeroboam had led Israel to commit' (I Kings 15.26, 34; and at the conclusion of the accounts of other rulers of the northern kingdom), in particular the building of shrines to rival the temple in Jerusalem. Chronicles describes the history of the northern kingdom from the perspective of Judah and so sees the disruption in which Israel was divided into two as an act of rebellion by Jeroboam who usurped the northern kingdom from the legitimate Davidic ruler. As the northern kingdom continued to be ruled by those who were not of David's line, it was considered to be a rebellious kingdom. In addition, only Judah maintained legitimate worship of God, so the practices of the

15

north serve 'no god' (these two points are made in the statement of Abijah in II Chron. 13.4–12).

The Greek version of Ezekiel has 190 in place of 390. If this is the correct figure, the exile of Israel would be counted from the fall of Samaria in 722 BCE. It is unlikely that a copying or similar error was made in the text; rather, each number was chosen to say something about the disruption of the relationship between Israel (the northern kingdom) and God. The figure 390 suggests that the disruption of its relationship with God took place when Israel ceased to acknowledge the kings of the Davidic line, Jerusalem as its capital city and the temple as its central place of worship. The figure 190 would accord well with history as we know it; that is, the people of the northern kingdom were exiled after the fall of Samaria in 722 BCE.

The passage refers to an incident in the life of Ezekiel, but the present account has been developed from a simple recollection of that incident. The statement in vv.4–6 assumes the accomplishment of the judgement on Jerusalem through siege (vv.1–2), and refers to punishment of the people in exile. The hope for a return of the two groups of exiles, from the northern and the southern kingdoms, suggests that these verses came from a period near the end of the exile.

Food in time of siege and exile

4.9–17

A fourth instruction to the prophet has to do with lack of food in the siege (vv.9–17). Grain for bread would be scarce so he had to make bread from a mixture of grains (v.9a). Bread and water would be rationed to small quantities each day, twenty shekels, about eight ounces or 227 grams of bread and a sixth of a hin, about one and a third pints or three quarters of a litre of water (vv.10–11).

An interpretation of vv.9a,10–11 in vv.16–17 shows that the shortages and rationing would be part of God's action against the people of Jerusalem. God would cut short the supply of bread and cause the people to waste away in their iniquity.

The instruction and its interpretation have been adapted and applied to the people's experience in exile by the addition of v.9b and vv.12–15. The command to make bread from a mixture of grains (v.9a) is followed immediately by a reference to the 390 days the prophet would lie on his side (vv.4–6) and have this bread for food (v.9b).

4.12–15 A new element, cultic impurity, is introduced here in the form of a dialogue between the prophet and God. The assumption is that, during the siege and exile, fuel as well as grain and water would be scarce, so the cake the prophet was commanded to make from a mixture of grains was to be baked on a fire made from human dung. This would make the food unclean, as human dung was ritually unclean (Deut.23.12–13). The prophet objected that he had never eaten anything that would make him unclean, and referred to various forms of unclean food forbidden in the law-codes of the Pentateuch. In response, God allowed the use of cow-dung which would not contaminate the food. The exiles were reminded to avoid those things which would make them unclean, even though they were in a foreign land where people were involved in what the religion of Israel defined as unclean.

They were to observe the law of God even in exile.

After the siege
5.1–4

The destruction of Jerusalem and the removal of its inhabitants is symbolically referred to in the command to the prophet to shave his head and face (v.1). The hair was to be disposed in three ways, to signify the fate of the people of Jerusalem at the end of the siege. By thirds they were to be burned, struck with the sword, and scattered to the wind (v.2); that is, all the people were to be removed from the city. The use of such imagery to signify judgement is also found in Isa.7.20.

This act of God in judgement on the people has been modified in v.3. A small number of hairs would be preserved by being bound in the hem of the prophet's robe, an action symbolising God's protection (compare I Sam.25.29) and showing that some people, a remnant, would survive through the action of God. The prophet was instructed to cast into the fire some (not 'others' as the REB translates) of this remnant, not to destroy them, as with the one third in v.2, but to purify them (through the *fire* of exile; compare 20.34–38). This constituted hope for the exiles. God would continue with them in their exile and through the purifying experience of that exile, seek to restore the relationship broken by Israel's disobedience. (REB follows the Greek text for v.4b. The Hebrew text adds 'from it will go out a fire to all the house of Israel', which suggests that the purifying of the fire would be for all Israel.)

The signs made clear
   5.5–17

A prophetic sermon directed against Jerusalem follows the last of the signs (vv.1–4). Jerusalem, favoured by God in its situation among the nations and by having God's laws and statutes, had rebelled against God and become more notorious in its wickedness than the nations (vv.5–6). God would therefore turn against the favoured one and bring on her the consequences of her disobedience.

God's indictment and judgement on the disobedient people are described and their consequences given in detail. The nations would see how God punishes the disobedient, and they would mock the ruined city (vv.8–9,14–15). The people would be reduced to terrible deeds of cannibalism and be scattered to the four winds (v.10). The latter point has taken up the symbolic scattering of hair to the four winds from v.2 and applied it to the people of Jerusalem. In v.12 the traditional threat of punishment; that is, pestilence, famine, the sword, and scattering among the nations has been put into the framework of the shaving symbol. The intensity of the threat leaves no doubt that Jerusalem would be destroyed and the people removed from it.

God's action against Jerusalem would make God known among the nations (v.13). God, who entered into a relationship with Israel which was characterised by obedience, was faithful to the relationship in the punishment of the disobedient people. The nations would see the actions of this faithful God and God would be known among them. Ezekiel saw what would happen to Israel as a lesson both to Israel and to the nations round about. This theme is taken up and developed in the discussion on Israel's history in ch.20 where the prophet gave God's concern for the 'honour of my name' (vv.9,14,22) as the reason why God did not destroy the people when they rebelled and were disobedient. The nations would know God by the way God dealt with Israel.

5.16–17   Words of judgement form the conclusion to chs.4 and 5. A new term, *arrows*, is introduced to signify the means of destruction, *deadly arrows of famine ... arrows of destruction*, but in the main the major points of famine (4.16) and destruction of the people (5.12) are taken up in a concluding summary. The final phrase, *I, the Lord, have spoken*, leaves no doubt that God was responsible for this judgement on the people.To the exiles this was a message that they had been judged and were going through the deserved punishment for their disobedience. They would also know themselves to be that portion of the people who would be saved by the action of God (5.3–4). It was for them a message of hope.

Judgement on the land
6–7

Judgement on the city of Jerusalem is extended to the *land of Israel* in chs. 6–7. This is connected to chs. 4–5 by reference to *sword, pestilence and famine* (6.11–12; 7.15) and leads in to the vision of the departure of the 'glory of God' in chs.8–11.

Judgement on the land of Israel
6.1–7

The word of judgement against Israel in vv.1–7 is identified *as the word of the Lord* (vv.1,2) and is presented as a speech direct from God (vv. 3–7). We can imagine the strong impact this would have had, which was increased by God's command to the prophet to *face towards the mountains of Israel and prophesy* (v.2). To *face towards* (literally, 'set your face towards or against') at the instruction of God is to turn the power of God towards a person or place. Similarly, to *prophesy against* is to turn the power of God's word against the people. Although *the mountains of Israel* are addressed (v.3), the word of God was directed against all Israel, as the addition of *mountains and hills, the ravines and valleys* shows.

Mountains may have been used to focus attention on the hills which were identified with much of Israel's apostasy (see Isa.2.14; 65.7; Jer. 2.20; 3.2,6; Hos. 4.13). However, the prophet spoke against cult places wherever they were be found (v.3). The shrines and all their paraphernalia would be destroyed and profaned. This refers to cult places set up for practices alien to the religion of the God of Israel. Not only were the places to be destroyed, but people of Israel would be killed and their bodies used to desecrate the altars and the idols (vv.4–6). In this way the alien cult would be removed (v.6) and the judgement of God brought against the people Israel. By this action Israel would know God is *the Lord* (v.7).

This statement of God's word of judgement suggests that the reform which took place under King Josiah in 621 BCE had not removed all alien cult shrines. Some may have continued to be used and there may have been a resurgence of alien cult practices after the death of Josiah, whose tragic loss at the hand of the Egyptian Necho may have caused people to lose faith in the reform and to revert to the old ways. The prophet spoke against these manifestations of alien cults. However, we are also to see in the words of the prophet a strong, general statement against Israel's past in which the people continually forsook God in favour of the worship of other gods. Israel's record of apostasy can be seen in the assessment of the kings of Israel and Judah in I and II Kings and the words of judgement from the prophets which extend from Amos in the eighth century to Jeremiah in the period immediately prior to the exile. Those who read these words after the fall of Jerusalem in 587 BCE were given clear reasons for God's judgement and punishment of the people in exile.

A remnant will repent

6.8–10

Words of hope for the exiles have been added to the judgement of vv.2–7. The exiles are explicitly referred to as *those that have survived the sword and are scattered in foreign lands*(v.8), but who had not been forsaken by God. God would deal with their *wanton and wayward hearts* with the result that they would *remember* God and *loathe themselves* (v.9). This means the people would repent, and turn away from their *idols* and *abominations*, because they recognised that God was faithful and would fulfil what was promised, even the evil to be inflicted on them (v.10). This was the beginning of hope for those in exile.

Judgement on those far away and those near at hand

6.11–14

6.11–12   Here we have further words proclaiming total destruction of the people of Israel. The prophet was commanded to *beat* (strike) his *hands together and stamp* his *feet*, actions which expressed God's anger and rage at Israel's acts of apostasy. Because of their actions they would fall by *sword, famine, and pestilence,* all of them, whether they were near or far away. What was said to be the fate of the people in Jerusalem (5.2,12) has been applied to all the people of Israel in terms of total destruction.

6.13–14 returns to destruction of the cult places in terms which are similar to those used in vv.4–6. It shows that the judgement to fall on Israel (vv.11–12) would result from the cultic apostasy of the people. Again there is a connection with the general apostasy to be seen in Israel's history as shown in the phrases *every hill or mountain-top, under every spreading tree or leafy terebinth,* which are to be found in the books of Kings, Jeremiah, Hosea, and in other places in Ezekiel. (See, for example, I Kings 14.23; II Kings 16.4; Jer.2.20; 3.6,13; Hos.4.13.) The *sweet-smelling sacrifices* suggests that the gods were pleased by the odours which came from the burning of sacrifices. God had already rejected these as a means of maintaining the relationship with Israel (Lev.26.31).

Total destruction was promised. (The text should read 'from the wilderness' [in the south] 'to Riblah', [in the north] rather than *more desolate than the desert of Riblah* as REB.) When it was achieved, the people would know that God is the Lord (v.14); that is, recognition of God came from acknowledging the actions of God. The 'recognition formula', 'you (they) *will know that I am the Lord*', occurs frequently in chs. 1–39. It states clearly that the people should be in no doubt that what the prophet declared as a coming event in the life of Israel would result from the action of God. It also made clear that God would be known by Israel and its neighbours by the way God dealt with Israel, for God's actions were consistent with the nature of God and with the relationship between God and Israel. The occurrences of the 'recognition formula' were frequent invitations to the people to see the hand of God in what had happened to them and to acknowledge the faithfulness of God in dealing with them. This pointed forward to the faithful God who would forgive, restore and renew when the people repented.

The end is coming
7.1–9

The judgement and punishment of ch. 6 are carried on in sayings about *the end* in ch. 7. It begins in vv.2–9 with a complicated passage

which appears to have gone through a process of expansion, interpretation and adaptation in arriving at its present form. This is
indicated by the difficult Hebrew text and apparent repetitions in vv.
2–4 and vv. 5–9. The Greek version omits parts of the text, especially
from vv. 5–6, and rearranges the remaining verses, putting vv. 6–9
between vv.2 and 3. The result is to harmonise what may have been
two parallel 'poems'.

7.2–4   The first poem, addressed to the *land of Israel*, says that the
'end' was near. It would be the end of the whole land (v.2). The *four
corners of the earth* refers to the world, but, in this context it is
intended to convey that the end would encompass all of Israel.

The use of the word *end* recalls Amos' vision of a basket of ripe
fruit and the play on the Hebrew words for 'summer fruit' and 'end'
which became for Amos a proclamation of the end of Israel (Amos
8.2). There is about the Amos statement a sense of the inevitability of
what was to happen which is also found in these words of Ezekiel.
God would *neither show pity, nor spare* Israel (v.4). Rather, God would
call Israel to *account for your conduct* and *bring all your abominations
upon you* (v.3). We should follow the Hebrew text and translate,
'upon you', rather than *on your own heads* with the REB. *On your own
heads* would suggest a change of address from the 'land' (singular) to
the people, which does not occur in the Hebrew. However, the close
relationship between land and people is to be recognised. The
people's *conduct* and *abominations* would bring the 'end' to the land,
thus negating the promise of God to Abraham and his descendants
that the land would be theirs (Gen.12.1–3;15;17).

7.5–9   The second poem directed the words of *doom* to the *dweller in
the land* and so made explicit what was implicit in vv.2–4, the end for
the land and its people. As a later development of vv.2–4, this poem
directed the declaration of the end to those who remained in Judah
and Jerusalem after the fall of Jerusalem in 587 BCE. It therefore
suggests that the continuing 'people of God' were to be found in
exile in Babylon.

The tradition of the 'day of the Lord' is recalled as the prophet
spoke of 'the day' as near, and the description *a day of panic and not
rejoicing* (v.7). Amos warned the people that the 'day of the Lord' for
which they longed, would not be a day of light, but a day of
darkness (Amos 5.18–20). That is, they looked for the day of God's
blessing but, because of their disobedience, it would be a day of

God's judgement on them (see also Amos 8.9 and Zeph. 1.14–18). It was a tradition which proclaimed God's determination to make a complete end to the disobedient people.

Destruction and end
7.10–27

The remainder of the chapter continues the themes established in vv.2–4, 5–9, the 'end' and the 'day of the Lord'. It does so in an impersonal way, using third person plural pronouns to indicate the object of the statements about judgement and doom. The Hebrew is again difficult, but the main points are clear.

The people were told that *the day* was coming, indeed, *doom is here*. The reason was *injustice*, which is like the bud on a stem, and *insolence* which bursts like blossom from the bud (v.10). They surely deserved doom and end (v.11).

7.12–16 Consequences of the coming of *the day* are given in vv.12, 14, and 15. First would be the suspension of normal feelings and reactions. For example, in trade there would be no sorrow that a sale had been made nor joy that a purchase has been obtained (v.12) and, even though they were threatened, they would not fight those who came against them (v.14). Second, they would be destroyed by *sword, pestilence and famine*, the means of destruction for the people of the city (5.12,16–17), and of the land (6.11–12). An explanation of how the threefold destruction would come on the people emphasises that all would be destroyed, those in *city* and *country*. There would be no escape. God's wrath was against all (vv.15b–16).

7.17–19 The description returns to the terror of 'the day' in v.17. It would produce weakness, they would not be able to lift their hands, nor would their knees be strong enough for them to stand (v.17). There would be mourning, with all its signs of *sackcloth, shuddering*, shamed-faces, and shaved heads (v.18, following Hebrew text. REB *sackcloth, shuddering from head to foot, with faces cast down and heads close shaved*), and despair as they cast aside what would normally be valued, their silver and gold (v.19).

7.19–20 The sign of despair, flinging away silver and gold, became the point of departure for a further explanation of why the calamity

would befall the people. They had disobeyed God, therefore the
wrath of God would come upon them. They would not be saved by
their *silver and gold*, nor could their riches provide food on that day.
Their downfall would come because of their iniquity in using their
precious things to make *vile, abominable images*.

7.21–24 Reference to silver, gold and jewellery in vv.19–20 leads to
discussion on how the people would be plundered by the oppressors
God would bring against them. God is presented as speaking in
these verses, but the people are not addressed directly, they continue
to be referred to in the third person. The effect of this is to express
God's distance from a disobedient people on whom the judgement
of God must inevitably fall.

Everything in vv.21–24 speaks of rejection. The people would be
plundered. God's face would be turned from them, a sign of dis-
favour and rejection, and the land defiled. God would create con-
fusion, let ruthless nations *take possession of the* people's *houses, quell*
their *pride* and *profane* their *sanctuaries*. The sense of rejection is
heightened by the description of the plundering nations. They
would be foreigners, most evil nations, brigands, and *ruthless nations*.
Those who knew a relationship with God would be destroyed by
peoples whom God saw as thoroughly objectionable. God's people
were even worse than they. Surely there could be no hope for them.

7.25–27 The description of terror continues. There would be no
peace, that is wholeness and well-being, for the people. Everything
that would give this – health, wealth, and the society of their people
– would be taken from them (v.25). Those to whom the people might
look for comfort, assurance of the presence and care of God and for
hope would be of no help – not prophet, nor priest, nor elder (v.26).
So even the comfort of their religion, which is promised in Jeremiah
(Jer. 18.18), was denied by Ezekiel. Their disobedience had put them
in a position where such comfort was not forthcoming, such was the
gravity of their actions. Nor would the secular leaders be of any help.
They would share the mourning and terror of the people (v.27a). *The
king will go mourning* may be an addition to the Hebrew text as it is
not in the Greek text. However, it may be that both 'king' and
'prince' are used to indicate that all officials would share the lot of
the people. For the people of the land there would be no help 'on that
day'.

These sayings of the doom and threat associated with 'that day' conclude with the statement that God would be responsible for the horrors the people would experience. In this action of judgement the people would be called to account for their apostasy and by the same action and judgement, God would be known to them (v.27).

A vision – the glory of God leaves the temple
8–11

These chapters are presented as the record of a vision which came to Ezekiel. They begin with a description of the prophet who, in a vision, was caught up and transported from among the exiles to the temple in Jerusalem (8.1–4) and they end with the prophet returned to Chaldaea among the exiles (11.22–25). Major additions have been made to the vision account. In chapter 10 an attempt has been made to link this vision with the account of the vision of God's glory in ch.1, and ch.11 adds another vision to the account (vv.1–13) as well as an independent statement about those who remained in Jerusalem during the exile (vv.14–21).

Transported to Jerusalem
8.1–4

The account begins with a date which puts the occasion one year and two months after the inaugural vision as recorded in 1.2 (taking 'the month' of 1.2 to be 'the fourth month' of 1.1). On that day the prophet was in his house with *the elders of Judah*. Visits from the 'elders' ('of Israel') are also mentioned in chs.14.1; 20.1, from which it appears that the elders came to the prophet to consult him. Whatever was happening was interrupted when *the power* (Hebrew, 'hand') *of the Lord God* fell on the prophet (v.1) and he received a vision from God (v.3).

Description of the vision begins in the second part of v.3 where we are told that a spirit carried the prophet to Jerusalem and set him down at the inner north gate. The 'man-like' being described in v.2, with his action in physically grasping the prophet's hair, emphasises the reality of the experience. However, vv.2,3a appear to be an addition made to connect this vision with that in ch.1 through its similarity to 1.26b,27. Verse 4 is also an addition made to serve the same purpose. That is, the presence of God, known in the prophet's inaugural vision in the 'glory of the Lord', was also known in this later vision of the temple in *the glory of the God of Israel*.

The first abomination
8.5–6

In the first part of the vision the prophet was shown an *idolatrous image* (literally an 'image of jealousy'), before which people were committing abominations; that is, practices which were associated with pagan religions and therefore loathsome to a true worshipper of the God of Israel. It is not known what the image was, but there is a suggestion in the use of 'jealous' (REB 'idolatrous') in the description that it was an object set up as a rival to Yahweh, the God of Israel. There is a play on the characteristic of the 'jealous God' of Exod.20.5 and Deut.4.24 in the account. The image was a sign that the people had rejected God who, as the 'jealous God', had to reject them. This rejection would cause God to leave the temple.

The second abomination
8.7–13

The description of the way by which the prophet saw the second abomination is complicated. Comparison with the Greek text suggests there have been additions to the Hebrew text, and the Hebrew word for *dig* may be better translated as 'investigate' or 'look carefully'. The description is then of the prophet being led to the gate of the court which surrounded the palace and the temple, shown the entrance, and commanded to go in and look at what was happening.

Inside the court the prophet saw pictures or relief carvings on the walls of *vermin, and all the idols of the house of Israel* (v.10). *Vermin* were various living creatures designated unclean in Leviticus (7.21; 11.10,12,20). *Figures of creeping things, beasts* is an explanation of what is meant by *vermin*. It has been incorrectly put before the word it is intended to explain.

Standing before these pictures, that is, worshipping them, were *seventy elders of Israel*. The use of the number seventy is significant. It recalled the seventy elders who were with Moses as representatives of the people in the covenant-making ceremony (Exod.24), and the seventy who shared with Moses the government of the people (Num.11.16–25). That is, representatively, all Israel was involved in the cultic disloyalty which this scene presents. The enormity of the situation is thus emphasised; all the people of God were involved in apostasy from God.

This may be an example of adoption of Egyptian worship in Jerusalem, as the description of the figures on the wall suggests Egyptian characters. Also, at the time overtures were being made to Egypt to assist Israel towards independence.

Those involved in these practices believed that God had left the land and it was in the control of others, so God could not see what they were doing (v.12). *In the darkness* is an addition intended to give further reason for God not seeing what the men were doing, but its inclusion takes away from the force of the statement that already God had forsaken the land and the people.

The third abomination

8.14–15

A further sign of gross disloyalty was shown to the prophet when he was taken to the north gate of the temple court. There he saw women *wailing for* an alien fertility deity, *Tammuz* (v.14), who was known in the Mesopotamian area from early times. His life cycle was related to that of vegetation in the seasons of the year. He died and went to the underworld in summer when the land was dry, in spring he was freed from the underworld by his sister Ishtar to bring new life which appeared with new vegetation. His death was a time of ritual mourning by women.

This abomination showed that Israel's religion had come under Babylonian influence, for the people were denying that God was the one who gave the produce of the land (compare Hos.2.8). It was a sign of gross abomination and disloyalty, but there was worse to come (v.16).

The fourth abomination

8.16–18

Finally, the prophet saw the greatest abomination of all, for in this, rejection of God was portrayed within the inner court of the temple itself. In the inner courtyard, at the door to the temple, twenty-five men (Greek twenty), possibly priests, were worshipping the sun. The description emphasises the enormity of what these men were doing. In order to worship the sun they turned toward the east and away from the temple, the place of the divine presence, away from God (v.16).

A question to the prophet raised the issue of this catalogue of abominations. Were they *a trifling matter?* (v.17). The answer may be seen in three statements that follow the question. It may have been given indirectly in the statement of God's intended action against the people, to *turn on them in my rage and show them no pity, nor spare them* (v.18). *They have filled the land with violence* may have been an answer that was added to show the seriousness of the people's position, pointing to their social transgressions, but it is out of place in this recital of cultic sins. The final sentence in v.18 may have been an answer but to what it refers is uncertain. It may have been some pagan form of worship (putting vine twigs to the nose), and so emphasise the acts of abomination referred to earlier. The Greek translators appear to have interpreted the phrase by translating 'turning up the nose'. This would be understood as a derisive gesture toward God and showed that the abominations could not have been thought of as trifling matters. Certainly the statement of Yahweh's intended action shows they were not trifling (v.18).

God orders destruction of the people
9.1–11

The account of the vision continues into the next phase in which God called on seven men to execute punishment on the people of Jerusalem. This narrative is presented with great skill so that there is a build up of dramatic tension from the announcement that those who would punish the people had arrived, to the end when the report that the task was completed was given. Its effect on the people must have been to strike terror in their hearts.

9.2-3   The men came from the north along the way the prophet had been brought in his vision. Six of them carried instruments of destruction (*battle club*) while the seventh, who was dressed as a priest (Lev.16.4), carried writing instruments with which to mark the righteous (v.2). The six were to function as destroying angels, similar to those referred to in II Sam.24.16 and II Kings 19.35. The whole

account is similar to the Exodus story of the destruction of the eldest
sons of the Egyptians, which also included preservation of those
who had been designated by God (Exod.12).

9.4–5   God, whose presence was acknowledged in *the glory of the
God of Israel* (see 1.28), directed the man dressed in linen to *mark with
a cross the foreheads of those who groan and lament over all the abominations practised* by the people (vv.4–5). The *cross* was the Hebrew letter
'taw', the last letter of the alphabet, written in the time of Ezekiel
as 'X'. That provision should have been made to spare some of the
inhabitants of Jerusalem shows that there were people in the city
considered faithful to Yahweh. Beyond the description, *those who
groan and lament*, the text gives no indication of who they were. From
what we know of the situation in the city at that time there are three
main possibilities.
   1. The Zadokite priests who were exempted from the charge
against the temple officials of having gone 'astray from me' (44.15);
   2. Jeremiah and those who supported him;
   3. Those who would soon be taken off into exile and who were
later seen to be the means through whom the 'people of God'
survived the calamity of the destruction of Jerusalem and the temple,
the loss of the king and removal from the promised land.
   From the direction to the man dressed in linen to *go through the city
of Jerusalem* and mark those who would survive the destruction
(vv.4–6), it appears that it was the people of the city who were taken
into exile who would be saved from the slaughter.

9.6–7   The destroyers were ordered to kill everyone whose forehead
did not bear a mark, beginning with those in front of the temple
whose dead bodies would be used to *defile the temple*. It was no
longer fit to be God's sanctuary, nor a place of refuge for those who
sought safety in the presence of God. All those who had rejected God
in their disobedience were rejected.

9.8–10   One of the functions of the prophets was to intercede
with Yahweh on behalf of the people (see I Sam.12.19; Jer.15.1;
Ezek.14.14). Ezekiel's reaction to the mass slaughter of the people of
Jerusalem was to ask if all would be killed. God replied that the
situation was so bad that all must be destroyed. He would *show no
pity* (v.10). However, when the man dressed in linen returned to
report that he had carried out his orders, there is the suggestion that

29

a remnant remained. This may be an implicit reference to the exiles, especially with the strong statement against the inhabitants of the land and the city in vv.9 and 10. Verses 8–10 indicate the state of all who remained in Jerusalem and Judah. There could be no future with them. The future was with those whom God had saved.

Destruction by fire
10.1–7

There has been considerable expansion of the vision in ch. 10. To the simple account of the instruction to the man dressed in linen to take coals from the temple and scatter them through the city, that it may be destroyed by fire (v.2), has been added a lot of detail about the cherubim on which the throne of God rested (compare 1.26). This is very close to ch.1, and is intended to form a link with that vision account. The prophet, who had received his call in a vision of the 'glory of God', in this further vision proclaimed the massacre of the people of Jerusalem, the destruction of the city and the departure of the 'glory of God' from the temple.

To complete the punishment, the city would be destroyed. The source of destruction would be from the temple itself, from the embers *lying among the cherubim*. Above the cherubim was the throne of Yahweh (vv.1–2). The cherubim were intercessors in some ancient world religions. In the Old Testament they are associated with the altar, and served to emphasise the majesty of God (I Kings 6.23–28; 8.6–9).

10.3–5   Associated with the destruction of the city was the preparation for the departure of the *glory of the Lord* from the temple. The exact positioning of the cherubim is not clear, but the *glory of the Lord* moved to the terrace of the temple. The signs of *the glory of the Lord*, *cloud* and *radiance*, show that the Lord had not yet left the temple (v.4; compare I Kings 8.10–11).

10.7   The final act in the destruction of the city was set in motion by one of the cherubim, a guardian of the holy fire, who put some of the fire into the hands of the man dressed in linen, who then left to carry out his orders.

This is a further statement of Yahweh's judgement on and rejection of the people. Not only would the wicked people be destroyed;

the city, that symbol of their relationship with God from the time of David, also would be destroyed. The destruction was decreed by God and would proceed from the temple, the place of the *glory of the Lord* (vv.2,4,7). The enormity of the situation was thus set before the people. Their faithlessness would cause the destruction of the very thing which God had provided for the maintenance of the relationship between God and Israel.

More on the cherubim
   10.8–22

Apart from vv.18–19, this section is a further attempt to link the vision in chs.8–11 with chs.1–3 by the identification of the cherubim with the 'living creatures' of ch.1. Comparison of vv.9–17 with 1.15–21 and vv.20–22 with 1.6–9 shows how similar the accounts are, and confirms the author's desire to associate the two visions which make important statements about God and the nature of Israel's relationship with God.

Verses 18–19 continue the account of the departure from the temple of the *glory of the Lord*, which moved from the terrace to the east gate, the main entrance to the temple. The final part of this process of departure is described in 11.22–23, which, apart from some repetition in 11.22, is a continuation of 10.18–19.

In his vision the prophet saw the destruction of people and city. The final rejection of Jerusalem and the faithless people was seen in the departure of God, in the form of the *glory of the Lord*, from the temple; that is, the people would be left in no doubt that they had been rejected by God.

A further vision of iniquity
   11.1–13

Although this vision has been placed within the temple vision of chs. 8–11, it is a new vision which is outside the sequence of events recorded in chs. 8–10. The substance of the vision is similar to that found in ch.8, but the prophet is said to have been transported to the temple (v.1) although he was already there according to chs. 8–10.

The vision came to be part of this complex because the prophet is said to have been transported by a spirit to the east gate of the temple, apparently from some place outside the temple area, probably Babylon. This is similar to 8.3 which commences the vision narrative in chs.8–11 with reference to *a spirit* which *carried/brought* the prophet to the temple. There is also a connection through the reference to the east gate which was the place where the 'glory of God' rested as it moved from the temple (10.18–19).

In this vision the prophet saw an act of disloyalty to God perpetrated by *twenty-five men* who were leaders in Jerusalem (compare ch.8). Two of the men are named and described as having *high office* (literally, 'princes of the people', v.1). Although they are not known outside this chapter, they must have been known in Jerusalem prior to the destruction of the temple in 587 BCE. The men were engaged in a meeting from which *mischief* (iniquity) and *bad advice* (counsel of evil) would come (v.2), which suggests they had responsibility for the plight of the city.

The words from the men, quoted in v.3, are difficult to interpret. The Greek version has interpreted the first part of the statement as a question, 'Have not houses been built recently?' This suggests confidence on the part of the leaders that the city would continue, with the assurance that God would not allow it to be destroyed. Protection is then the point of the second part of the statement. The city is like a cooking pot which holds its contents and in a sense protects them. The following verses then deny the correctness of the assumption and turn the saying back on the men who said it (vv.4,6–7).

The weakness of this interpretation is that the image of the cooking pot is one of cooking, of breaking down the contents, not one of protection (see 24.3–6).

As v.3 is translated in REB it is a statement of the situation as the men saw it. They were in a time of threat and felt themselves contained in the threatened city like meat in a cooking pot, so it was unwise to be building houses. Their planning would then be concerned with how to handle this situation. We do not know what they planned but, in what follows in vv.4,6–7, it is clear that it was contrary to God's plan for the city.

11.4 The prophet was commanded to prophesy against the men and to lay the blame for the situation at their feet. They are depicted as the cause of Jerusalem's plight, not the saviours of the city. At this point we notice a significant difference between this vision and what was seen in ch.8, where the temple, which was the focus of the worship life of the people, and the sign of God's presence with them in Jerusalem, had become the place where the disobedient people participated in alien cult practices. That is, the disobedience was cultic in nature. In this vision the disobedience was social, communal and political in nature, and took place in the city. The addition of this vision to chs.8–10 shows that God judged the people of Jerusalem because their disobedience was to be seen in all spheres of life. It also shows that the people were required to be obedient to God in both their cultic life and their community and political life. They were responsible to God in all areas of life.

11.5 The words of judgement took up the actions of the twenty-five men in planning and offering advice, and their statement. However, the judgement was against the whole people, as *you men of Israel* (literally, 'house of Israel') shows. All were involved in the disobedience. The twenty-five were representative of the people Israel.

11.6–8 The charge was that the people had caused death, therefore they would be punished by being driven from the city, by the *sword* which would be brought against them, and by being handed over to a foreign power (v.8). Reference is made to the saying in v.3 by asserting that the victims of those who planned were the meat, and the city the cooking pot which had been the effective container for those slain (v.7). However, those responsible would not escape, rather, they would be driven from the city.

11.9–12 Additions to the text have developed the words of judgement in terms of events of 587 BCE. Leaders of the people were taken to Riblah to the north of Israel, which may be seen as the fulfilment of the prophetic word (vv.9–10; see II Kings 25.18–21). The second addition refuted the words of the men in the gateway (v.3) and affirmed that the judgement would come on the people because they had not been obedient to the *statutes* and *laws* of God, but had followed the laws of other nations (v.12). By this judgement the people would know God.

11.13 The vision concluded with the death of Pelatiah, one of the two officials named in v.1. This was seen as confirmation of the words of the prophet. However, as the name means 'God delivers', the death may have been interpreted by the prophet as a sign that there would be no remnant from the destroyed city and caused him

33

to cry out in appeal to God. Would God make a complete end to the people Israel? It was an act of intercession by the prophet on behalf of his people.

A word of hope for the exiles
11.14–21

This was originally an independent oracle of hope for the exiles and not part of the temple vision. It has became part of the vision complex because it gave an answer to the cry of the prophet and because it identified the exiles as the people in whom the hope of Israel rested. The saying is in the form of a claim by the inhabitants of Jerusalem (v.15) and a refutation of that claim by the prophet (vv.16–21).

The inhabitants of Jerusalem laid claim to the land vacated by those taken into exile because the exiles were *separated far from the Lord* (v.15). This statement represents the traditional view that God and the land were so associated that separation from the land meant separation from God (see I Sam.26.19; Hos. 9.3). Thus the punishment of exile meant separation from God and loss of the land God had given Israel. Those who remained in Jerusalem and in the land God had given their ancestors therefore thought of themselves as the sole inheritors of the land, and the people through whom God would restore Israel.

Some hint of the reply given in v.16 had already been given in the phrase *this whole people of Israel* (v.15). By referring to the exiles in this way, the prophet designated them as the continuing people of God in whom the hope of Israel rested. The reply acknowledged God's responsibility for the situation of the exiles. God removed them to the distant places but they were not removed from God, who was with them in those places (v.16), as the words *for a little time I became their sanctuary* shows. Verse 16 brought together two things; the understanding of a sanctuary as a place of meeting with God and the message of the vision that God's presence was withdrawn from the sanctuary (used of the temple in 8.6; 9.6) in Jerusalem. Thus the people in Jerusalem were told that their assumption was false. They remained in the land but God had forsaken them and they therefore could not consider themselves to be the inheritors of God's promise of the land. On the other hand, the exiles were told that God's presence was with them even though they were in exile, and that presence would be known to them in the distant place as it had been in the temple in Jerusalem. This was a clear statement that God had not cast off the exiles, but, rather, they still figured in the purposes of God.

11.17   gives another reply to the words of the people of Jerusalem. The exiles were addressed directly and assured that they would return from the lands of exile to *the land of Israel*, which God would give to them. This again refuted the claim of those who remained in Jerusalem and established the exiles as the rightful possessors of the land, even though they were separated from it.

11.18   while conveying the fact that the religion of the returned exiles would be purified, is also an indictment of the people in Jerusalem. They were not fit to be the possessors of the land because they had maintained the vile and abominable practices which the returning exiles would have to remove. The word of comfort to the exiles has been applied to those who remained in Jerusalem; they would have to *answer for all they have done* (v.21).

11.19–20   In contrast to the indictment of those who remained in Jerusalem, there is promise for the exiles who would be renewed to the depths of their being. The promise of *singleness of heart* and *a new spirit* expresses this. (Greek has 'another' for 'singleness', which would require a minor alteration to the Hebrew text. The difference between the two words in Hebrew is one easily confused letter. The Greek text fits well with the second half of the verse and is closer to the parallel passage in ch.36.26, which has 'new'. 'New heart and new spirit' occur together in chs.18.31 and 36.26.) The further statement that their *heart of stone* would be replaced by a *heart of flesh* is a powerful image to make the same point. The *heart of flesh* would be able to respond to God and enable the people to live by the *statutes* and *laws*. The covenant relationship would again be God's gift to the renewed people – *They will be my people, and I shall be their God* (v.20)

It is important that we notice here that renewal was through the action of God. The people would be changed and obedience to the law would become their response to the God who had renewed them. The passage as a whole makes it clear that renewal was available to the exiles, not to those who remained in Jerusalem who were considered to be involved in disobedience.

The end of the vision
11.22–25

The vision account concludes with the description of the departure of the *glory of God* from the city (vv.22–23) and the return of the prophet to the *exiles in* Babylon [*Chaldaea*] (vv.24–25). As noted above, this is a continuation of 10.18–19 from which it was separated with the insertion of 11.1–21. The point made in vv.22–23 is that the *glory of God* not only departed from the temple, it also went from *the city* leaving both temple and city without the assuring presence of God and depriving the people of the sign that they were God's people.

When the vision ended and the prophet was again aware of his presence among the exiles, he told them all that had come to him in the vision. The import of the vision for them was that they could not take hope in Jerusalem which was condemned by God and would be destroyed. Rather, they should acknowledge that, even though they had been judged and were being punished in exile, yet God had spared them, was with them and would renew them. The vision as a whole is therefore a statement of hope for the exiles and an indication that hope for a disobedient people would come through judgement, punishment and renewal by God.

False prophets
12–14

These chapters have a central theme of prophecy and the demonstration of the truth of Ezekiel's prophetic words and actions. There is some polemic against those who presented a false hope, which confirms the faithfulness of Ezekiel as a messenger of God.

Journey into exile
12.1–16

Ezekiel was commanded to act out a prophecy in the sight of the people as a sign to them (v.6). He was reminded that they were *a rebellious people* whose rebelliousness prevented them hearing and seeing what God revealed to them (v.2. Similar statements are found in Isa.6.9; 43.8; Jer.5.21. See also on 3.7, pp.8f.). The intention of the acted prophecy was that, when the people saw the action of the prophet, they would realise their condition and repent (v.3).

The prophet was told to prepare to go into exile by collecting the few things that could be taken on the journey, then to leave home, as if going into exile. This was to be done in the presence of the people, a recurring point in the passage (vv.3,4,5,6,7), to emphasise that the action was to be a sign to them. It was also a play on the charge that the people *have eyes and see nothing* (v.2) and, *it may be they will realise they are rebellious* (v.3). This has been taken up again in the later interpretation concerning the prince (Zedekiah) who *cannot ... see* (v.12; see below).

12.5–6   The further command to the prophet to *break a hole through the wall*, leave in the *dusk* and cover his face as if in disguise, appears to belong to a later stage of the text as it refers to escape from the city rather than going into exile. It is a reference to the escape of the prince (v.12). Similarly, *so you cannot see the ground* is a reference to the blinding of the prince (vv.6,12).

12.8–11   gives an interpretation of the prophetic action. The people's inability to 'see' was emphasised by their need to ask Ezekiel what he was doing (v.9). His answer would be that, in acting out preparation to go into exile, he was a sign to warn the people of what was to come to them (v.11) and to say that the exile was the action of God against them. This was addressed to those who were still in Jerusalem, but it also reminded the exiles that their plight was the result of God's action. Their punishment was the consequence of their disobedience. By this prophetic action the realisation of the truth of their situation became harder to escape.

12.12–15   is a second interpretation applying the prophetic action to the 'prince', Zedekiah, who attempted to escape from Jerusalem at the end of the siege applied by the Babylonians. The description is closely related to the account in II Kings 25.4–7 and Jer.39.4–7. The concluding formula, *they will know that I am the Lord, when I disperse them among the nations ...* (v.15), confirms that those who were in exile were there because of the work of God.

12.1–15   may also bear the interpretation that there was no escape from exile, a point that is emphasised in v.16, the conclusion to the passage as a whole. God would preserve some of those who went through the destruction of the city, the survivors of *sword, famine, and pestilence*, who would be taken into exile and through whom the nations *among whom they go ... will know that I am the Lord* (v.16). This was a message of hope to the exiles who were to be seen as the survivors and those with whom God continued to work.

Threat of destruction
   12.17–20

A further acted prophecy is given in v.18 and interpreted in vv. 19–20. The prophet's action in eating with trembling and drinking with shuddering (v.18) recalls the anxiety and dismay of the people over food and water shortages during the siege of the city (4.10–11,16–17). There were still things to fear in the action of God against the people.

12.19–20   The interpretation shows that the prophetic action was directed against the people of Jerusalem. The exiles had to understand that destruction would come to the city because of the disobedience ('violence') of its people. Everything would be destroyed, and in the destruction the exiles would know *that I* (God) *am the Lord*. The exiles did not have a source of hope in the city of Jerusalem, nor in its inhabitants.

What God has said will happen
   12.21–28

Two sayings, which are very similar, conclude ch. 12. They were not originally connected to vv.17–20, but now carry forward the point of the earlier verses – God's word would be fulfilled.

The prophet had heard that people were using proverbial sayings to show that God's word would not be fulfilled (vv.22 and 27). In the first saying it was suggested that the prophet's words (*visions*) would not eventuate because they had been spoken in the past (v.22) and were no longer effective. The second suggested that the words applied to the distant future (v.27). The prophet dealt with each saying in the same way by proclaiming that the time of fulfilment was near (v.23), and that the word spoken by God, through the prophet, would be fulfilled (v.25). It would not be delayed (vv.25, 28).

These sayings tell us that the prophetic words were intended to be heard in terms of the immediate future of the people, but, even if fulfilment was delayed, it would still come. There was no room for false hope by the people; the purpose of God in judgement would be achieved. God is shown to be faithful in the words spoken by the prophets. When God promised judgement, judgement would come and the people of Jerusalem could not interpret delay as escape from judgement. Similarly, when the prophet spoke of hope, it was on the same understanding of the faithfulness of God. Realisation of hope might be delayed, but it would come. This was an important reassurance to the exiles.

Against false prophets
13.1–23

The two sayings which conclude ch.12 lead into statements against false prophets (13.1–16), and women who prophesied falsely (13.17–23). Each of these statements contains two sayings against those charged, with parallels between the corresponding part in each statement.

This chapter shows the seriousness with which the prophets' words were viewed as messages from God and highlights the difficulty people had (and still have) in determining the authenticity of the prophetic word; a point that is recognised in Deut.18.21–22, which, in effect, says that the proof of authenticity is in the fulfilment of the saying. The same point is taken up in Jeremiah, first in his confrontation with Hananiah, the prophet from Gibeon, who refuted Jeremiah's words of doom and destruction with words of peace (Jer.27–28), and second, when he wrote to the exiles in Babylon to deny the words of the prophets who spoke of an early end to the exile and a return to Judah (Jer.29).

We are reminded also that there were many prophets in Israel's history who claimed to speak the word of God. Those who were recognised as authentic prophets, who often had to speak unpopular words to the people, had to contend with those who spoke popular words. The authentic prophets claimed that those who opposed them with popular words did not speak the authentic words of God.

13.2. Ezekiel's prophetic statement began with a claim to an essential difference between what he said and what the so-called *prophets of Israel* said. Ezekiel received from God the command to speak and the words to be spoken. The other prophets spoke for themselves *from their own minds.*

13.5–7 develops the charge against the false prophets. Ancient cities depended on their surrounding walls to protect them from enemies so it was necessary to ensure they were always in good repair. Any breach in the wall had to be repaired. The false prophets, with their false words were like people who refused to do this and so left Israel open to the action of God *on the day of the Lord* (v.5). The suggestion is that they had betrayed their people into judgement and punishment with their false visions and divinations (v.7).

13.8–9 The prophet pronounced God's judgement on the false prophets with the words, *I have set myself against you* (v.8). As with the earlier verses (vv.4,6,7b are additions), this statement has had added to it words of punishment for the false prophets who would be excluded from the people of Israel (v.9). They would not be part of the community, nor numbered among the people of Israel, nor return to the land of Israel. Therefore they would be excluded from Israel's hope in God, having no part in the restoration of the exiles to their land nor in the renewed national life.

13.10–16 gives a further charge and statement of judgement, which takes up again the thought of the wall (similar to v.5). In this case the wall was not a substantial structure, but rather a wall of loosely fitted stones without mortar. The false prophets covered it with whitewash (v.10) which may have given the appearance of strength, but God's action in wind and storm would soon prove that it was appearance only when the wall was destroyed (v.13). The actions of the false prophets would do nothing to preserve an Israel threatened by the judgement of God because they gave messages which prevented the people from seeing themselves as the disobedient people of God. This has been made explicit by the additions in vv.14–16.

God would be known in the action taken against those who spoke falsely about God's actions against Israel (vv.9,16).

13.17–19 The second set of sayings against women who prophesied (vv.17–21,22–23) has parallels to the sayings in vv.1–9,10–16. Their prophecies *come from their own minds* (see v.2), but Ezekiel was commanded to speak by God (v.17). The charge in particular was against the practice of a form of sorcery in which the practitioners attempted to control the lives of people (v.18), which is well known wherever sorcery and magic are practised. The *magic bands* and *veils* were objects used to enable the magic to work. A later addition in v.19 interpreted this in a more prophetic way by saying that these 'prophets' were telling the people what they wanted to hear, which was lies.

13.19–21 As with the earlier passage, the charge was that these 'prophets' claimed to act at the direction of God, but Ezekiel said their actions *dishonoured* God and were for their own gain (v.19). The result of this was that the people were told what they wanted to hear and were not brought to face the reality of their situation as the dis- obedient people of God and, therefore, were unable to make the decision God required of them. God's action against these 'prophets' would be to remove their implements of magic, the signs of their power, and so free the people from their power (vv.20–21).

13.22–23 The second saying accused these 'prophets' of reversing the way that God acts through the prophets, for they *undermined the righteous* and *strengthened the wicked* (v.22). The result would be that they would all perish under God's judgement, whereas God meant the righteous to be encouraged in their lives and the wicked to be convinced to turn to obedience to God, and thus become righteous. This is a statement similar to the one on the 'watchman' (3.16–21), which emphasised that the prophet's task was to warn the people of the judgement to come if they persisted in their disobedience. The prophet who did not fulfil that task would be judged, as would the women to whom the prophet referred who did not warn those in danger.

As with the previous saying, God's punishment for the prophets (male and female) would be to prevent them from using their powers, and to rescue the people from their influence (v.23). This effectively nullified the power and influence of the false prophets.

Judgement on idolatry
14.1–11

14.1–3 A visit to the prophet by *the elders of Israel* became an occasion for the prophet to address the state of the religion of the people in exile. The exiles were living among the victorious Babylonians whose gods may have been considered more powerful and, therefore, more effective than their God, who was the God of a conquered people far from their homeland. That some of the exiles succumbed to the influence of the Babylonians is clear from the words of the prophet (v.3).

The visit by the elders provoked a question about the appropriateness of God receiving an inquiry from people who had been unfaithful by worshipping *idols* and being involved in *sinful things* (v.3). It seems to assume a negative response, that is, it was not appropriate to answer, but God would answer (v.4) with a statement of judgement on the unfaithful people (v.8). The terms used in this judgement show that people who were guilty of idolatry would be cut off from God and from God's people. This was in effect the pronouncement of a death sentence.

14.4–8 The structure of the response (v.4) was given in the form of 'sacral law' which is very similar to that found in the Holiness Code (Lev.17–26). In particular, the indictment and judgement form (vv.7–8) corresponds to parts of the Holiness Code (for example, Lev.17.10–12; 20.2–5). The occurrence of this form suggests that Ezekiel was aware of the Holiness Code (Lev.17–26) and used it to show that the people had broken the established law of God. Indeed, it recalls the most heinous form of idolatrous practice, child sacrifice (Lev.20.2).

A call to repentance has been added in v.6, emphasising that the purpose of God's action against the people was that they should repent. It also picks up two terms used frequently in Ezekiel and descriptive of Israel's acts of disobedience to God; *idols*, a derogatory term, the Hebrew of which may be translated 'dung idols', and *abominations*, cultic and ethical acts which were loathsome in the sight of God. The two terms together spoke of the people's rejection of God. Ezekiel called his people to 'turn' from this disobedience. Verses 7 and 8 return to the legal form. Verse 7, which is very similar to v.4, presents a situation in which God would take action against an Israelite or resident alien who renounced God for idols, and v.8

gives the judgement of God which was to cut off that person from the community of God's people.

14.9–10   The case of a prophet who gave an oracle to an idolatrous inquirer is discussed in this addition. For the prophet this could be only a case of God misleading the prophet (v.9) with the consequent destruction of both prophet and inquirers (v.10). A similar way of dealing with the situation is given in Deut.13.1–5 which describes the way prophets who attempted to lead the people astray to other gods were to be treated; that is, they were to be put to death. Deuteronomy also explains that God was testing the people through the prophet, so the people should ignore the prophet's signs and remain faithful to God (Deut.13.3–4). Two instances of prophets who claimed their harmful or deceitful words came from God as tests for people are found in I Kings 13 and 22. For Ezekiel, the understanding that God was the source of all prophecy was maintained and the responsibility of God for the punishment of Israel reaffirmed.

14.11   The conclusion looked to the punished, repentant and purified people to be faithful to God. The covenant formula, *they will be my people, and I will be their God*, summarised and confirmed this and established the link with the traditions of Israel on which Ezekiel drew, and to which he was faithful.

Intercession and impending judgement
14.12–23

A second discussion in legal form is given in vv.12–21. The form is of the 'case' type, in which a case is introduced with a condition; for example, 'if ...', and followed by a judgement introduced as a consequence, such as 'then ...'. This form is found in many places in the Old Testament; for example, Lev.20.9–21; 25.35–38; Deut.21.18–21; 24.1–7; Ezek.14.4.

In this application of the form, the traditional four expressions of judgement and the futility of expecting that even righteous people of great fame could avert that judgement from a sinful nation are stated. Thus, when God promised to send *famine, wild beasts, the sword, and pestilence* against a sinful nation (vv.13,15,17,19), the presence of Noah, Daniel and Job in that nation would be of no advantage in saving it (vv.14,16,18,20). Their righteousness would

43

save them, but it would be of no avail in saving others, not even a son or a daughter.

The righteousness of Noah, Daniel and Job was proverbial, not only among the people of Judah, but also in the traditions of other peoples. Noah is portrayed in Gen.6–9 as God's faithful person who acted at God's direction in the great flood. A similar hero figure, who was righteous and wise, is found in the flood stories from the Mesopotamian area and would be known to the exiles in Babylon.

The spelling of the name 'Daniel' (possibly 'Danel'), found only in Ezek.14.14; 28.3, suggests that Ezekiel was not referring to the person presented in the book of Daniel, but rather to a Phoenician, the father of Aqhat, who is depicted in a poem from Ugarit as a wise and righteous ruler whose judgement assured the rights of widows and orphans. The association of this Daniel with the ruler of Tyre in Ezek.28.1–3 suggests this connection with Phoenician traditions is correct.

Job is known to us from the biblical book of that name who is identified as a man from Uz (Job 1.1), the location of which is unknown but which has been traditionally associated with Edom. The story of Job was well known in the ancient Near East. Job is included here because he was a righteous man who overcame all obstacles and finally achieved vindication.

That the presence of such wise and righteous people could not save Israel is in contrast to the account of Abraham's discussion with God over the fate of the notoriously wicked city of Sodom. God agreed that the city would be spared if as few as ten innocent people could be found in it (Gen.18.16–33), but in this later case, the righteous could save only themselves. This indicates the seriousness with which the prophet viewed the sinful state of his people. They were worse than Sodom (see also on Ezek.16.44–63).

A similarly serious view of the state of Israel's relationship with God was given by Jeremiah, who, after interceding for his people, received the answer from God that not even such noted intercessors as Moses and Samuel could save Israel (Jer.15.1–2).

The prophets were aware of the importance of intercession, but they were also aware there were times when the people had put themselves beyond the benefit of the prayers of their intercessors. The only thing that would save the people addressed by Ezekiel was repentance, not the presence nor the intercession of righteous individuals among them (compare this with Ezek.18, and see below on that chapter).

Israel is not named in vv.12–20, but it is clear that Israel is the nation to which the prophet referred. In verse 21 the general charge is made specific in words of judgement against Jerusalem, which would suffer all the four forms of punishment against people and animals listed in vv.13–20. The exiles were to know that judgement and punishment would result from faithlessness, which both explained why they were in exile and reminded them of the need to be faithful while they were in exile. It also pointed to further judgement against Jerusalem because its people continued to be disobedient.

14.22–23 A later development of the text says that some people would survive the terrors and destruction as the exiles had done. It is a message of hope to the exiles who were survivors of the destruction of Jerusalem and, therefore, people with whom God continued to deal.

The vine
15

This short chapter proclaims the utter destruction which would befall Jerusalem as the result of God's judgement on the faithless people. They were as useless as a scrap of charred and burned wood. Destruction was inevitable.

The charred vine branch
15.1–6

The chapter is in two parts. In the first part, vv.1–6, the prophet asked four questions about the value of a piece of wood from a vine. First, how does it compare with other timber brought from the forest (v.2)? Second, is it useful for making anything? Third, can it even be used as a peg (v.3)? Fourth, is it any good for fuel, especially when it has already been partly burned (v.4)? The questions are not answered immediately, but all four are answered in v.5, where it is said that the wood cannot be used to make anything, especially when it has been charred.

The second part of the chapter applies this discussion to *the inhabi-*

tants of Jerusalem (vv.7–8). As charred vine wood is fit only for the fire, so *the inhabitants of Jerusalem* would be consigned to the fire, even those who were left in the city after the first deportation of 597 BCE. They could not escape the coming judgement (v.7). It was the consequence of their faithlessness (vv.6–8).

In presenting this indictment and its consequences, the prophet drew on the traditions of Israel in which the vine, the fruit of the vine, and the vineyard were used as symbols for Israel. When Moses sent spies into the promised land to determine its quality and the strength of its inhabitants, they returned with a bunch of grapes so large it needed two men to carry it (Num.13.17–24). The prophets Hosea, Isaiah and Jeremiah used this symbol to show that Israel was unfaithful to God. Hosea described Israel as a 'luxuriant vine' yielding fruit which the people used in alien cult practices (Hos.10.1–2). Isaiah likened Israel to a vineyard which was prepared and planted with great care but which yielded wild grapes. He said Israel, like the vineyard, would be destroyed (Isa.5.1–7). Jeremiah also likened Israel to 'a choice vine' which became 'a wild vine' (Jer.2.21).

Ezekiel took up the tradition in his own way. He emphasised the wood of the vine rather than its fruit, which enabled him to stress that Israel had become worthless in the purposes of God, because of its faithless disobedience. The traditional theme as a symbol of fruitfulness became the means of describing the utter uselessness of the inhabitants of Jerusalem (v.6).

A further use of the tradition of the vine is found in John 15.1–14. This draws on the uses found in the Old Testament and thus appropriates the traditions to the followers of Jesus. It develops the thought in the direction of the Christian's life being sustained by participation in the life of Jesus Christ.

Judgement on Jerusalem
15.7–8

These verses are an addition to the oracle which has two purposes. First, to declare to the *inhabitants of Jerusalem* that although they had escaped deportation in 597 BCE, they would not escape the coming punishment and, second, to declare that when Jerusalem was destroyed, God would be known in that action. For the exiles after 587 BCE this would be an assurance that God had acted in accordance with the covenant relationship with Israel.

An alternative is to divide chapter 15 at the end of v.5. This sees vv.2–5 as a saying of the prophet, with vv.6–8 as an interpretation of a parable. It is suggested that the style of vv.6–8 differs from vv.2–5, and 'therefore' (not in REB) is a sign of an addition to an existing piece of material. A further possibility is that v.6 is a first addition and vv.7–8 a second, and later (exilic) addition.

Taken as a whole, ch.15 states that the exile of Israel was the act of the God of Israel, who judged and punished a faithless and disobedient people. Those who had not experienced the judgement had not avoided it; because of their continued disobedience, judgement for them was still to come.

The unfaithful foundling
16

Chapter 16 begins with a graphically told folk story about a foundling which the prophet has used to present the condition of favoured but faithless Jerusalem. This theme is used to develop a charge of apostasy against Jerusalem in the first part of the chapter (vv.1–43a). The second part of the chapter (vv.43b–63) also deals with apostasy, but does so through a comparison between Jerusalem and her 'two sisters', Samaria and Sodom. (See the Introduction, 'Sexual language, imagery and metaphor', pp.xvii–xix.)

The foundling who became unfaithful
16.1–43a

Within vv.1–43a the theme of the foundling is developed in a number of sections which proceed through charge, judgement, and punishment. The sections contain words from the prophet and later developments of those words made to give them greater impact and application to Israel's ongoing experience in its relationship with God.

The folk story is applied immediately to Jerusalem with a statement about the foundling's parentage. The reference to her *Amorite father* and *Hittite mother*, along with her birth in Canaan, recalled the origin of Jerusalem, which became an Israelite city after its capture by David. However, the terms have a pejorative sense in other places, so

their use here makes a derogatory statement about Jerusalem's beginnings, which correspond to her later history. Her origins were foreign
and her later practices were alien to the relationship with God.

16.1–14 The account tells of the finding of a newborn and helpless
child who had been left naked, unwashed, lying in her blood and
uncared for (vv.4–6), imagery which has been taken up in the
account of the judgement at the end of the narrative to emphasise the
forsakenness of the disobedient woman (vv.37–39). The child was
taken and cared for by God and, when she grew to be a beautiful
woman, God entered into a covenant with her and provided her
with fine clothes, jewellery and food. Arrayed in all her finery, she
was famed throughout the world for her beauty, and it was God
who had made her so.

The purpose of the story was to show that Jerusalem, and the
people of Israel as a whole, had received unmerited favour from
God. Indeed, there are parallels between the story and the history of
Israel. God saved Israel from destruction at the beginning of her life
in the exodus from Egypt, cared for her and provided for her in
every way, and put all this within the framework of a relationship in
which God sought a response of love and loyalty.

16.15 shows that God's expectation was not fulfilled. Instead of
love and loyalty to God, the beautiful and greatly favoured one
turned to others and offered herself to them. She spurned God's love
and turned away from the relationship which was God's gracious
gift to her.

16.16–22 The indictment found in v.15 has been developed further.
Four specific charges relating to the use of God's gifts in the service
of other deities were brought against Jerusalem. The clothes were
used to *deck the shrines* where she offered herself (v.16), and to cover
images to which she also gave the food God provided (vv.18,19).
Gold, silver and jewellery were used to make idols (v.17), and even
the children God had given were sacrificed to the images (vv.20–21).

These separate charges gave details of the general charge that
Jerusalem forsook God in favour of other gods. This was expressed
in the fertility cults of the Ba'als and child sacrifice to the god
molech, both of which were abominations in the sight of God and had
been condemned by the prophets Hosea and Jeremiah (Hos.4.11–15;
Jer.3.1–20; 19). There was also a recollection of Hosea's charge that

Israel did not know that it was God who gave her the gifts which she enjoyed (Hos.2.8–9). Jerusalem had forgotten God who gave her life and sustained her in life.

16.22–25 The charge in these verses follows on from v.15. Jerusalem was involved in cultic apostasy, setting up shrines in prominent places and furnishing them for cultic prostitution. The harlotry referred to (v.15) covers both the wanton disregard of God and the cult, and actual cultic prostitution. The terms *couch* and *shrine* refer to items of other cults and so make explicit that Jerusalem had forsaken her God for other gods.

16.26–29 records a change from cultic apostasy to political apostasy. Jerusalem was accused of being unfaithful to God by her alliances with foreign powers, the Egyptians (v.26), the Assyrians (v.28), and the Chaldaeans (v.29). The charge against Jerusalem was thus broadened. She was called to trust in God in all aspects of life, even for protection against enemies, as is shown in Isaiah 7. Any attempt to seek other aid was a sign of disloyalty and disobedience to God and a reason for judgement and punishment. The catch words *harlot* and *harlotry* connect this charge with what has gone before.

16.30–34 shows the enormity of Jerusalem's disloyalty. The actions of Jerusalem in seeking alternatives to God are likened to a prostitute who paid those who came to her rather than expecting payment for her services. Jerusalem could not claim to be a victim of circumstances. She was the initiator of her actions and relentless in her pursuit of her aims. The indictment is clear. Jerusalem had paid tribute to foreign powers to gain their assistance, but this betrayed her loyalty to God.

This reinterpretation of the theme of disobedience is similar to Hos.8.9–10; 12.1, and may owe something to the Hosea tradition. The connection with the original material in ch.16 is established through use of the key words *couches, lofty place, harlotry* and *lovers*. The charge of apostasy is thus expanded, and the reason for judgement and punishment confirmed. There can be no doubt that Israel deserved judgement and punishment.

16.35–41 give the statement of judgement and punishment. By taking up terms found in the indictments, they make it clear that judgement was a consequence of Jerusalem's actions and must be followed by punishment. Punishment would come at the hands of the *lovers* whom Jerusalem had cultivated in alien cults and foreign alliances, and is described in terms of the punishment of an adulteress. At the end of the punishment Jerusalem would be as she was at the beginning, *stark naked*, without *clothes, jewellery* and *shrine* (vv.35–37a,39–40).

This central statement has been developed by the addition of further details of the punishment to be brought against the faithless one. In this process it has been generalised to include *murder* as part of the charge (v.38) and destruction of houses as part of the punishment (v.41a). The whole statement has been made to apply to the sinful city (nation) as it existed throughout history and to the final destruction which was its punishment for continued disloyalty to God.

16.41b–43a   A conclusion has been added to show the effect of God's judgement on Jerusalem and to draw a lesson from the story (vv.41b–43a). God would end Jerusalem's apostasy (v.41b), and conclude her punishment (v.42). A summary in v.43a drives home the point that there was no hope of avoiding the punishment; God had to act against the disobedient people, but the hope that the punishment would have an end remains (v.42).

Jerusalem and her notorious sisters
16.43b–58

A further charge against Jerusalem was laid through comparison with her mother, a Hittite, and her sisters, Samaria and Sodom, all of whom were unfaithful to their husbands and children (v.45). Jerusalem was more guilty than her sisters because she *surpassed them in depraved conduct* (v.47), indeed, *they appear innocent by comparison* (v.52). This is further emphasised in vv.53–58. Jerusalem made her notorious sisters appear righteous, and even became a source of comfort to them.

The traditions concerning Sodom and Samaria were recalled because they told of the notorious behaviour of the two cities, and of their destruction by God. Jerusalem's destruction at the hands of the Babylonians was to be seen as an inevitable consequence of her behaviour.

The passage is connected to vv.1–43a by the reference to

Jerusalem's ancestry and the theme of unfaithfulness. It was a development of that passage, drawing on the proverb, *like mother, like daughter* (v.44), the traditions about Sodom (Gen.13;18;19; Isa.1.9–10; Jer.23.13–15) and Samaria (Jer.23.13–15; Hos.7.1; 8.4–7; 10.5–8; Amos 4.1–3; 6.1–7), and the folk story of two faithless sisters (Jer.3.6–10; Ezek.23.1–35). All of these traditions emphasised judgement and punishment on those who were disobedient to God. Their use here confirmed the message of vv.1–43a. The destruction of Jerusalem and the exile of the people were acts of God which inevitably followed Jerusalem's persistent disobedience.

Hope beyond judgement
  16.59–63

Finally, a message of hope has been added to the words of judgement and punishment, which does not deny the need for such actions by God (v.59), but sees them as the means by which the faithless one would be brought to repent (*remember ... and feel ashamed*, v.61). God would then 'pardon her' (v.63) and re-establish the *covenant which will last forever* (v.60, also v.62).

This concluding statement is connected with what has gone before. It recalls the beginnings of Jerusalem *when you were young* (v.60), which takes us back to vv.8,22,43; and the comparison between Jerusalem and her two sisters in vv.43–58 (v.61). Two points in the previous material are reversed in this conclusion. Jerusalem had not 'remembered' in the time before her disobedience and punishment (vv.22,43), but she *will remember* (vv.61,63). The disgrace and estrangement Jerusalem suffered (vv.53–58) would be removed when God established with her the *covenant which will last forever* (v.60).

Chapter 16 as a whole was a powerful and moving sermon of hope for the exiles. It identified the reason and rightness of their punishment, which enabled the exiles to recognise why they were in exile; it proclaimed God's continuing care for the people, the desire that they should repent, and readiness to forgive and restore them when they repented.

The parable of the eagles
17

Chapter 17 is introduced with an instruction to the prophet to give the people a *riddle* and a *parable*. The two words are used to describe a fable or story in which animals or plants speak and act like people. There is behind the story an important meaning for the people.

The story is given in vv.3–8, followed by two questions to draw out its meaning (vv.9–10) and two interpretations which apply the story to the relationship between God and Israel as reflected in the fall of Jerusalem and the experience of exile (vv.11–21 and 22–24).

The story of the two eagles
17.1–10

The *great eagle* (v.3) represents Nebuchadrezzar in his power and glory. The *cedar tree* in Lebanon is a term of honour for the Davidic line of kings, and the *twig* taken from the top of the cedar refers to Jehoiachin, who was taken to Babylon (*land of traders*) by Nebuchadrezzar in 597 BCE.

The remainder of the story refers to Zedekiah, also of the Davidic line (*a native seed*), but considered a regent rather than a king. Hence he is described as a vine, *low along the ground* and dependant on Nebuchadrezzar, *bending its boughs towards him … its roots growing beneath him* (vv.5–6).

The second *great eagle* refers to the Egyptian Pharaoh to whom Zedekiah appealed for assistance against Babylon (Jer.37.5–8). When the assistance came it was too late and of no benefit to the besieged Jerusalem. The appeal is depicted as the vine twisting its roots and trailing its boughs toward the second eagle (v.7).

The questions in v.9 invite certain conclusions from the story. The vine which had changed its allegiance could expect only destruction presumably from the first eagle. Confirmation of this assumption appears to be the aim of the addition in v.10 with its reference to *the east wind*, suggesting Nebuchadrezzar.

The interpretations
17.11–24

The interpretations make it plain that the story, although it did not specifically refer to Jehoiachin and Zedekiah, was their story in the time of Zedekiah's reign in Jerusalem. Verses 12–15,19 probably comprise the first interpretation, to which was added more specific reference to the fate of Zedekiah in vv.16–18,20–21, and a final interpretation of hope in vv.22–24.

The first interpretation makes the important point that Zedekiah was a vassal prince under Nebuchadrezzar, bound to him by treaty and oath (v.13), which should have resulted in faithful service to the Babylonian king, but Zedekiah rebelled against him (v.15). In these circumstances Nebuchadrezzar would be expected to act against his rebellious vassal with punishment and destruction, an action which was shown to be appropriate by God's oath *As I live*, ... and the promise of retribution on Zedekiah. The destruction promised to Zedekiah would also be God's retribution on him, for he had not only broken his oath to Nebuchadrezzar, he had also brought dishonour to God, in whose name he would have been required to swear the oath (v.19).

The remaining verses in vv.11–21 have been introduced to bring the interpretation up to date following the fall of Jerusalem and the removal of Zedekiah to Babylon and so emphasise that God had brought the promised retribution on the disobedient king. There is close similarity between vv.20–21 and 12.13–14.

17.22–24   A final interpretation, using the terms and imagery of the story but emphasising hope, has been added here. In this it is God who will act, not an eagle, and the *tender shoot* will be exalted, not humiliated, when it is planted on *the highest mountain in Israel*. It is a messianic promise which used the story to give hope after the judgement of vv.1–21 rather than another interpretation of the story.

Responsibility before God
18

Chapter 18 interrupts the two statements on kings in chs.17 and 19 to deal with accountability before God in terms of individual responsibility. The discussion also raises the question of whether the generation in exile was responsible for what had happened to them, or were previous generations to blame? It may have been placed between chs.17 and 19 to make some comment on the last kings of Judah prior to the exile; if so, the kings would have demonstrated the point made in ch.18.

The passage is introduced with the quotation of a proverbial saying (v.2) and developed in the form of a disputation in what follows. Objections by hearers are given in vv.19, 25 and 29 and the discussion is concluded with a statement of judgement from the prophet (v.30).

18.2–4   The proverb quoted in v.2 was evidently a popular saying in the time of the exile, as its quotation in Jer.31.29 suggests. The proverb indicates that the people believed they were suffering for the sins of their parents as they applied the words of Exod.20.5 ('punishing the children for the sins of the parents to the third and fourth generation') to their experience of exile. This led them to see the reason for the exile as the disobedience of previous generations, but the prophet refuted this when he said, *parent and child alike are mine. It is the person who sins who will die* (v.4; compare Jeremiah's treatment of the proverb in Jer.31.30).

In what follows the prophet showed that a person suffers the consequences of what he or she has done (vv.5–20), and he stressed that repentance by a sinful person would bring forgiveness only to that person (v.21–23).

18.5–9   The first case considered was of a righteous man who was pronounced righteous because he conformed to the statutes and loyally observed the laws of God, so *he will live* (v.9). In the detailed consideration of the righteous man's actions, the prophet listed thirteen laws or prohibitions observed by the man (vv.5–8). Similar lists are given in the second and third cases that follow, and in the Psalms (for example Pss.15; 24.3–6), which suggests they were part of the temple ritual and were used as a means to determine the righteousness of a person. Such a person would be pronounced righteous with a formula such as, *He conforms to my statutes and loyally observes my laws* (v.9 and, indirectly, v.17).

There is no list elsewhere in the Hebrew scriptures which coincides with those given in ch.18, but individual items in the lists occur in the major law codes. For example; adultery (v.6), which is prohibited in the Ten Commandments (Exod.20.14; Deut.5.18) and the Holiness Code (Lev.18.20; 20.10); oppression (v.7), the Covenant Code (Exod.22.21) and the Holiness Code (Lev. 19.13,33); returning the debtor's pledge (v.7), the Covenant Code (Exod.22.26); and regarding money lending (v.8), the Covenant Code (Exod.22.25) and the Holiness Code (Lev.25.36). In discussing righteousness, the prophet drew on the established traditions of the people as given in the law codes of Israel.

18.10–13   The second case is of the son of the righteous man who was the opposite to his father; that is, unrighteous. Most of those things which the father refrained from doing, the son did, the others not being mentioned. The conclusion, that *because he has committed all these abominations he must die* (v.13), shows that the son was judged on the way he lived his life. The righteousness of his father could not save him from the consequences of his actions.

18.14–17   The third case is another reversal of the position. The unrighteous man had a righteous son who observed the laws his father had disobeyed, and was like his grandfather. The conclusion was that he should not *die for his father's wrongdoing; he will live* (v.17).

18.18–20   is a summary statement of the principle involved in the three cases. The judgements on the three men were based on what each of them had done. The righteousness of a father could not save a disobedient son, nor could a righteous son save a disobedient father. Each one had to bear his own judgement. The righteous one lives, the sinful one dies.

18.21–24   The argument is carried on a further stage as the prophet considers the effect of a change of heart by the righteous and the sinful. Repentance by a sinful person would result in life, not death; that is, repentance would bring life (vv.21–22). In this is revealed God's attitude to sinful Israelites. God desired their life, not their death, so their past offences would not be held against them (vv.23–24). Conversely, the righteousness of one who turned to disobedience would not avert the judgement of death (v.24).

18.25–29   The same point is discussed here, but in the reverse order. Here the reply is given to the charge that God *acts without principle* by stating that God's action was in accord with the principle that the righteous would have life, but the wicked would have death.

18.30–32   In the conclusion the prophet took again the point that each person would be judged *on his record*, and called on the Israelites to repent, rid themselves of their past misdeeds, and get *a new heart and a new spirit*. In this context the *new heart and new spirit* are what would result when a person turned away from wickedness. The command to *get* a new heart and a new spirit differs from the promise of God's gift of a new heart and a new spirit in ch.36.26 ('one heart' in 11.19). The two forms highlight the action of God toward the people in calling for repentance, offering the way of repentance and renewal when the Israelites repented, and acknowledging that the person had to accept the opportunity to repent. It focuses the dynamic of the relationship between God and the person, and between God and the people Israel. God desired life for Israel, not death.

Lament over the rulers of Israel
19

This chapter, although in two parts (vv.2–9,10–14), is designated a lament (or dirge) in its opening and closing words (vv.1,14). It has the form of a lament with the characteristic two-line poetic structure in which the first line has three beats and the second two beats.

The lament was part of the mourning process in Israel in cases of death and other tragedies. David's lament for Saul and Jonathan is an example of a lament for individuals (II Sam.1.19–27). The book of Lamentations uses the form to mourn a national tragedy, the exile. Prophets used the form to point the people to future tragedy as they lamented over what was to happen to Israel, the disobedient people of God (see, for example, Amos 5.2; Jer.7.29;

8.18–23; 9.10–11). They also used the form to refer to the fate of other nations (e.g. Isa.14; Ezek.26–28,32).

A lament for two princes of Israel
19.2–9

The lament is presented in terms of a lioness and two of her offspring but identification of individuals who fit the description is difficult. One obvious possibility is Hamital, wife of Josiah, and her two sons, Jehoahaz, who reigned for three months after Josiah's death, and Zedekiah, who reigned for the last years up to the exile. Jehoahaz was exiled to Egypt (v.4; II Kings 23.31–34), and Zedekiah to Babylon (v.9; II Kings 25.6–7). However, Jehoiachin, who reigned for three months after the death of Jehoiakim before he was removed by Nebuchadrezzar and replaced with Zedekiah, was also exiled to Babylon (II Kings 24.8–15) and must be considered. He was not, however, a son of Hamital, nor her grandson. If the consideration is confined to vv.2–9, it appears most likely that Hamital and her two sons were the subject of the prophet's lament. If vv.10–14, which clearly refer to Zedekiah (see below), are taken with vv.2–9, the image is generalised, the mother becomes Judah, and the princes those who were part of the final process towards the exile of Judah; that is Jehoahaz, Jehoiachin, and Zedekiah. The lament in vv.2–14 therefore mourns not only the fate of these three kings, but also the end of the Davidic monarchy.

The imagery of the lion was characteristic of the kings of Judah (as decoration for the throne, I Kings 10.18–20; as part of the royal symbolism, II Sam.1.23; Prov.19.12; 20.2; and of the tribe of Judah, Gen.49.9.). Jehoahaz reigned for only three months and is condemned for his wrongdoing in the brief account of his reign in II Kings 23.31–33, but he is described in terms of the strength and prowess of a young lion (v.3) rather than what as a prince he achieved. Similarly, his imprisonment and removal to Egypt is in terms of the capture and transport of a lion (v.4).

The second part of the lament over the young lions (vv.5–9) is similar to the first, with the king being taken to Babylon and long-term imprisonment. Two kings of Judah's choice finished in exile.

A lament for Judah and its rulers
19.10–14

The image of the vine, already seen in chs. 15 and 17, has replaced that of a lion and its cubs in the second lament. In this presentation the *mother* (Judah) *was a vine* and *stout branches* represent the rulers of Judah (vv.10–11), all of which were destroyed when the vine was *torn up* and *blighted* by the *east wind* (Nebuchadrezzar, v.12).

The purpose of the lament was to show that Judah and the line of kings from David had ended, so the people could no longer look to them as a source of hope. To this has been added comments to identify Zedekiah's rebellion as the immediate cause of the end of Judah's existence (*fire burst from its own branches*, v.14), with his exile and the execution of his sons as the end of the dynasty (v.11b and v.12b, *its strong branches were blighted*, v.12). A further interpretation identified the fate of Judah as exile (v.13).

The enclosure of the two poems within opening and closing statements referring to a lament shows the final form of ch.19 to be a lament over the rulers of Israel. As such it takes up the negative attitude towards the monarchy found in other writings (Deut.17.14–20; I Sam.8.10–19; 12.16–22; Jer.21.1–7; 22.1–7; 23.1–4).

Reviewing Israel's history
20.1–44

Chapter 20 deals with the history of the people of Israel as a response by the prophet to an inquiry from *some of the elders of Israel* (v.1). The history is in two parts, vv.4–31, from the time in Egypt to the exile, and vv.32–49, God's release of the people from exile.
(Note. The paragraph divisions in REB suggest a division at v.36, but the change from looking back to the past to looking to the future takes place at v.32. Also, vv.45–49 are placed at the beginning of ch.21 in the Hebrew Bible.)

An inquiry
20.1–3

A group of elders visited the prophet in August 591 BCE to consult with him, but we are not told what matters they wished to raise.

Rather, the prophet was directed away from consultation (v.3) to deliver a sermon addressed to the exiles in which he recalled their history and charged them with continued disobedience to God (vv.4–31).

The historical recital is divided into sections which correspond to the major parts of Israel's history: in Egypt (vv.4–9), in the wilderness (vv.10–26) with a foreshadowing of the exile (vv.21–26) and in the land (vv.27–31). Arrangement of material within the sections follows a pattern which highlights God's action toward the people. God's favourable action towards them, provision of the way for response, lack of obedient response, God's decision to punish the people, punishment postponed and a new opportunity given. However, the conclusion in vv.30–31 showed that punishment for disobedience, which was postponed in God's earlier dealing with Israel, was being experienced by the exiles, the just punishment of a disobedient people. God would not be consulted by them.

In Egypt
20.4–9

The first period of history deals with the time in Egypt and the exodus. It recalls acts of God toward the people in their election and the revelation of God as their God, the promise of deliverance from Egypt and the promise of a land. It also states that God commanded the people to rid themselves of idols (vv.5–7). There is some difference here from the tradition in the Pentateuch in which the prohibition of idols was given in the Decalogue (Exod.20.3–17; see vv.4 and 5). In this Ezekiel is either telescoping history to make the point of his theme of the grace of God to which Israel's response was disobedience, or he was aware of a different account of the early traditions.

The people refused to heed God's command and clung to their idols (v.8). God's action against them for this disobedience in Egypt was forestalled that the name of God might not be profaned in the sight of the nations (v.9). For the people of Israel the name of a person expressed what the person was in his or her being. So, the giving of the name in Exod.3,6 gave the people some insight into the being of God. Also, when the writer of Deuteronomy wanted to avoid the suggestion that God was to be found only in the temple, he said that the 'name of God' was in the temple, signifying that God's presence was there, but God was not localised in the temple (Deut.12.5,11). The choice of Israel and the revelation of God's name (*I am the Lord your God*, vv.5,7), meant that God would be known by the life of the Israelites; that is, what God did with them and to them revealed the nature of God. To have left the people in Egypt would have shown God to lack faithfulness, and/or power to fulfil the promise made to the people. An essential part of Ezekiel's presentation of Israel's history was that God was faithful to the promises made to the people. When the people were brought out of Egypt, God was revealed to the nations, and the name of God honoured.

In the wilderness: the first generation

20.10–17

The wilderness period is dealt with in two parts. First, the rebellion of the people who were brought out of Egypt (vv.10–17), and second, the rebellion of their children (vv.18–26). Again God acted to provide for the people's response by giving *statutes* and *laws*, that in *keeping them ... mortals have life* (v.11), a reference to the law given at Sinai (see above on 18.9; see also Lev.18.5 for the legal form of this). 'Sabbaths' as a sign of the relationship were also given (v.12). Observance of the sabbath was important in Israel, as its place in the major legal codes of Israel indicates. The sabbath came to have particular significance for the exiles as one of the few ways Israelites could maintain their distinctiveness as God's people while in a foreign land.

Rebellion against God came in terms of disobedience to the *statutes* and *laws*, and desecration of the *sabbaths*. God resolved to punish the people, but again, as when the people rebelled in Egypt, punishment was withheld *for the honour of my name* (vv.13–14). However, there was a deferred punishment. God swore not to allow them to enter the promised land (v.15), but this stopped short of total destruction (v.17), their children were allowed to survive. This recalls the tradition that the generation which God brought out of Egypt would not enter the promised land, but perish in the wilderness (Num.14.28–32; Deut.1.34–39).

In the wilderness: the second generation
20.18–26

The children of those who were brought out of Egypt were charged as their parents had been. They were to *conform to* the *statutes* and *observe* the *laws, keep* the *sabbaths holy*, and keep from idols (vv.18–20), but they too were rebellious, and, although God resolved to punish them, again the punishment was withheld for the honour of God's name among the nations. However, as with the previous generation, God's action was qualified, they were promised exile for their disobedience (vv.23–24) which emphasised that Israel's exile was to be understood as the result of the disobedience and faithlessness of its people.

20.24–26   Further evidence of the exile as the result of the people's wilful disobedience may be seen in the prophet's statement that God gave malign statutes and *laws which would not lead to life, let them defile themselves with gifts to idols*, and *made them surrender their eldest sons to them*. This appears to refer to the law on the offering of the firstborn to God (Exod.22.29; 34.19) which the people interpreted as a command for child sacrifice. Such an interpretation would be against other laws which provided for the firstborn human to be excluded, for the child had to be redeemed and another appropriate offering made (Exod.13.13; 34.20). In particular, child sacrifice was explicitly forbidden in Deuteronomy (Deut.12.31; 18.9–10) and Leviticus (Lev.18.21; 20.2–3), and two kings, Ahaz of Israel and Manasseh of Judah, were condemned by the Deuteronomic historian for this practice (II Kings 16.3; 21.6). If Israel practised child sacrifice in compliance with the law for the offering of the firstborn, they would be defiled by a law God had given them but which they obeyed with disregard for other laws.

In the land
20.27–29

An addition, aimed at including life in the promised land in the recital of Israel's history, has been made in vv.27–29. The charge against Israel was apostasy from the cult. God had given Israel the land in fulfilment of the promise, but Israel had responded by becoming involved in alien worship at places associated with these

practices, hill tops and under leafy trees. In this they effectively
denied the relationship with God.

Verse 29 contains a play on words which the English translation
cannot reproduce. It depends on the sounds of the Hebrew words
for 'what',' go up' and 'hill-shrine' ('high-place'). The effect was to
scorn the *hill-shrine* and reduce it to a place of no value, as it was in
the sight of God.

Judgement
20.30–31

The address concludes with rhetorical questions to the elders
which related the sinfulness of their generation to the sins of their
ancestors. The questions show that the people in exile were seen to
be as sinful as their ancestors, therefore God would not be consulted
by them.

A new exodus
20.32–44

A new address begins with the quotation of a saying of the exiles
that they should become like other nations and *worship wood and
stone* (v.32). This reflected the despair of the people that they were far
from all that they thought essential to their religion and, therefore,
cut off from their God, which left them open to the influence of other
people's gods and religious practices. God's response to this was to
affirm by vow (*As I live*) responsibility for the people and to promise
action on their behalf, which is expressed in terms of God's continued reign over the people and ability to gather them from the
lands where they had been dispersed. The phrase *with a strong hand,
an arm outstretched* (vv.33,34) shows that God's action was to be
understood as a second exodus (see Deut.4.34; 5.15; 7.19; I Kings
8.42, where it is used of bringing the people out of Egypt) and
parallel to the action of bringing the people out of Egypt in vv.9–10.
A second wilderness experience was also promised to the people
(vv.35–36), an experience which would reflect that of their ancestors.
They would be judged as their ancestors were judged (compare with
vv.10–13) and purged by passing *under the rod, counting as you go*, a
shepherding image of the sheep entering the fold or enclosure

(vv.37–38), and a parallel to the denial of entry into the promised land by the rebellious first generation of those who were brought out of Egypt (v.38, compare v.15).

This was a message of hope to the exiles. The parallels to the earlier passage are deliberate as they show that the God who judged and punished Israel was also the God who would take them through the judgement and restore them to their land of Israel.

Verse 39 stressed that worship of idols would bring punishment, but there would also come an end to such practices by the Israelites. As such the verse appears to refer back to the purging declared in v.38. On the positive side, God declared that those who returned would offer worship at the place God stipulated (*my holy mountain*) and in the way God required, and that they, their worship and their service would be accepted. The positive nature of this is accentuated by the statement that *the nations will witness it* (vv.40–41).

20.42–44   A further word of hope emphasises that God would be known in the action of restoring Israel to its homeland, and that the exile was not only a time of punishment, but also an opportunity for repentance. So, as the action to judge Israel was required by the honour of God's name, the action to forgive and restore repentant Israel was required also by *the honour of* God's *name* (v.44).

The sword of destruction
20.45–21.32

When we look at vv.45–49 it is obvious that they belong with 21.1–7. Verses 45–49 present an allegory of destruction which has been interpreted in 21.1–5. The parallels between particular parts of allegory and interpretation show that the two belong together and have been incorrectly separated in the arrangement of chapters. The interpretation leads in to further sayings in which *sword* is the catchword.

The sword of God
20.45–21.7

20.45–48   In a three-stage command the prophet was instructed to address the south; that is, he had to face towards the south, speak towards the south, and prophesy to the scrubland of the south (REB *Negeb*, which is the name for a region south of Judah but here the word has the general meaning of *south*, as the parallels in the two previous phrases show). The impact of the action of the prophet was intensified by his use of the phrase *set your face towards* ..., which is an expression of threat, in this case against Judah (*the south*). The use of *south* by a prophet in Babylon, which is to the east of Judah, shows that Ezekiel was referring to an enemy who would approach Judah from the north. This would be the direction of approach by Babylon or other enemy from the Tigris-Euphrates region which would travel round the fertile crescent and then proceed southwards through Syria.

The words spoken in the address threatened total destruction of the scrubland (*all the wood, both green and dry alike*) by a fierce fire that would not be put out. In the destruction God's action would be seen.

20.49   provides a bridge between allegory and explanation in the quotation of words of the prophet's hearers: *He deals only in figures of speech*. The people could find excuse for not understanding the prophet's words if they were not presented in a direct way. So the explanation was given.

21.2–5   The interpretation identified each item of the allegory in terms of Israel and its experience of judgement. Jerusalem, her *sanctuary*, and *the land of Israel* were identified as the objects of destruction which a *sword*, like the fire, would consume. The sword was ready to be used against Israel and would never be put away. In this destruction, all would know that God had acted.

21.6–7   The message spoken by the prophet was so terrible that it demanded some expression of horror on his part. The prophet's bitter groan was his reaction to what was to come, and the anticipation of what the people would soon experience. It confirmed that God's judgement was upon the people.

The song of the sword
   21.8–17

Further sayings with *sword* as the catchword follow the interpretation of the allegory. The first (vv.8–17) is often known as the song of

the sword because of its poetic structure. It may have been an existing poem the prophet used to convey to the people the reality of the
threat of God's judgement against them. The original poem is in two
parts, vv.9b–11, 14–16, with an introduction (v.8a) and a conclusion
(v.17) to identify the poem as God's word of judgement to the
people.

The first part of the poem describes the readiness of the sword to
accomplish its purpose. *Sharpened to kill, burnished to flash like lightning, ready for the hand to grasp*, give a picture of an instrument of
terror ready to do the bidding of God. The second part takes this
further as it describes the slaughter brought by the sword and the
fear it would raise in the hearts of the threatened people.

The two parts are separated by words of sorrow for those who
suffered by the sword and referred in particular to the people and
rulers who were killed in the siege of Jerusalem and after its fall in
587 BCE. It strikes a different note from the exultation in the poem
itself (vv.12–13).

The sword of Nebuchadrezzar

21.18–27

21.18–24   The second saying is in the form of God's command to the
prophet to act out a sign to identify the sword of destruction with
Nebuchadrezzar. Ezekiel was told to make a map, and draw on it a
road with a fork in it and there place a signpost with one sign pointing to Rabbah in Ammon, and another to Jerusalem. At this signpost
the king of Babylon would consult diviners to determine which city
he would attack. Each of the methods of divination was well known
at the time and believed to give a sign of the will of a person's god.
The people the prophet addressed may have scorned this way of
seeking guidance (v.23), but it resulted in Nebuchadrezzar turning
towards Jerusalem to attack it, which agreed with God's judgement
on the city. There is a suggestion in this saying that the God of Israel
was in control no matter what method the king of Babylon chose to
determine his actions against Israel.

21.25–27   The words against the *impious and wicked ruler* refer to
Zedekiah, who rebelled against Nebuchadrezzar. He would be
deposed, as the removal of *diadem* and *crown* show, and everything
would be disrupted in the ruin God promised. The last part of v.27

suggests a guarded word of hope with the return of Jehoiachin, whom Ezekiel regarded as the true king of Judah, and with a recollection of Gen.49.10, which looks forward to the coming of a great leader.

A sword against the Ammonites
21.28–32

The third saying returns to the catchword *sword* to apply it to the Ammonites, who were said in v.20 to be worthy of judgement and destruction by the sword. The REB translation suggests that the words were spoken against the Ammonite god as well as the Ammonites, but *shameful god* is better translated 'their reproach'. This poem takes up the judgement proclaimed against Ammon in ch.25, and surrounding nations in 36.5, where it is said that they would be destroyed because they reproached or mocked Jerusalem at the time of its destruction.

21.30–32 After the command to *return the sword to the sheath*, the sword, which was the instrument of judgement, is addressed in terms of judgement and destruction. Its end would come at the hand of God, and by the means which it handed out judgement, it would receive judgement. The sword represents Nebuchadrezzar, who was the instrument of God's judgement on Israel and Ammon, and who would be destroyed by *barbarous men*. This latter comment may be a reference to the Persians, but it is more likely to be a general reference to what happened to a great power when it was defeated and taken over by its foes.

Against sinful Jerusalem
22

Further charges related to the theme of sinful Jerusalem have been brought together in this chapter.

The city of bloodshed
22.1–16

This charge is introduced in a similar way to that in ch.20 with God's question of the prophet, *will you bring a charge against her?* which,

when it was repeated and expanded, became a command to con-
demn Jerusalem (v.2). What follows differs from ch.20 by addressing
the sins of Jerusalem, rather than the sins of past generations.

22.3–5   The charge is in three parts. The first is in general terms and
accused the city of bloodshed and making idols which defiled it,
followed by an account of the judgement that would come in the
taunting and mockery from nations who would see the infamy of the
city and its consequent fall.

22.6–12   More detailed listing of the sins of people is given in the
second part. Three groups of people were accused of shedding
blood: *rulers of Israel* (v.6), *perjurers* (v.9), and those who *have accepted
bribes* (v.12). The rulers were accused of social and cultic sins, the
perjurers of cultic and sexual sins, and those who accepted bribes,
sins of property and commerce. Each of the sins listed is covered in
the law codes of Israel with many of them occurring in the Holiness
Code (Lev.17–26). As with ch.18, a list on which the prophet drew
may have been available.

It should not be thought that the prophet was attempting to give a
list which covered all the sins of Jerusalem. Rather, the list showed
that Jerusalem had turned away from God, as is seen in the return to
the general statement in the last words of the charge, *You have committed apostasy*, or, in a literal translation of the Hebrew, 'You have
forgotten me' (v.12). The list of offences shows that God was not
acknowledged by the people. It therefore served the same purpose
as the lists in Hos.4.1–3 and Jer.7.6,9; that is, to demonstrate that God
was forgotten, the people were apostate, therefore they would be
judged (vv.4b–5). Similar charges of 'forgetting' God are found in
Hosea (2.13;4.6 ['forsake' REB]) and Jeremiah (2.32;3.21 ['ignored'
REB];13.25;18.15), where they are associated with various acts of disobedience.

22.13–16   Two further words of judgement are given in the last part
of the charge. The first takes up the accusation of having *oppressed
your fellows for gain* from v.12 and promises God's action against the
people. The second promises the people will be scattered among the
nations that they may be cleansed (v.15), but it also threatens the end
of the nation of Israel. Cleansing appears to be taken up again in *I
shall sift you* ..., but an alternative (and preferred) translation, 'I will
be profaned because of you in the sight of the nations', shows the

enormity of Israel's disobedience. This was so great that God would allow the nation to come to an end, even though such action had been rejected when punishment of previous generations was considered (20.9,14,22).

The smelting furnace
22.17–22

The figure of the smelting furnace gave the prophet another way to tell the people that God's judgement would include them all. Behind the prophet's words is the method of smelting silver to purify it. Other metals and impurities were removed and thrown away as waste. When Ezekiel looked at Israel he saw not silver, but the waste product which had the appearance of silver. This is not clear from the REB translation which has *alloy* instead of the more usual term 'dross' and so obscures the sense of worthlessness which is fundamental to the prophet's thought. God's action would be like smelting with great heat; with *anger and wrath* God would melt them, and Jerusalem would be the site of the judgement.

The judgement in vv.17–22 has some similarities to the words of Isaiah, who spoke of God refining Israel as one refines silver (Isa.1.21–25), and to Jeremiah, who said that God could not separate the pure from the impure, so all would be rejected (Jer.6.27–30). It may also draw on the traditional statement that God brought Israel out of Egypt, 'from the smelting furnace' (Deut.4.20; I Kings 8.51; Jer.11.4), to show God's judgement as a negation of the exodus, and to suggest a return to captivity as in Egypt.

A land of corrupt leaders
22.23–31

The final charge follows the theme of the two that precede it: condemnation of the people and in particular their leaders. This is later material which was added to address the situation after the fall of Jerusalem and to justify God's action against the city (v.31). There are similarities between vv.23–31 and Zeph.3.1–4,8, suggesting that the author drew on Zephaniah's work.

Jerusalem's condition in the time of God's judgement was like a desert. Lack of rain was a sign of the wrath of God (v.24) which was aroused by the actions of five groups of people whom the prophet condemned. *Princes, priests, city leaders, prophets,* and *common people* were all charged with doing things which were against the way of God, and which showed their disregard of God. No one showed respect for what was required of the people of God. Again the point of general, all-encompassing disobedience was being made and there was no person among them who could change the way the people were heading (v.30; see 13.5, where what God sought is listed as the task of the prophet).

The sermon ends: they got *the punishment they deserved*, which is a suitable end to the chapter which stated clearly why God had judged the people. It explained to those in Babylon why they were in exile and warned them of the need to be obedient to God.

The unfaithful sisters
23

A folk-story of two sisters and their unfaithfulness was used to bring charges and judgement against Samaria and Jerusalem for their political alliances with Egypt and Assyria, with whom they were accused of 'playing the whore' and acting as 'harlots'. The charges are similar to those based on the story of the foundling in ch.16, where Jerusalem's cultic apostasy was called 'harlotry'. In both cases the people were seen to be unfaithful to God as they turned to other gods or to neighbouring nations. (See 'Sexual language, imagery and metaphor', in the Introduction, pp.xvii–xix.)

The story of two unfaithful sisters
23.1–21

The immoral actions of the sisters were traced back to Egypt (vv.2–3). It is not known what may be referred to here, but it presents the same view as in 20.8, that Israel was unfaithful to God from the beginning of the relationship. The names *Oholah* and *Oholibah* appear to be related to the Hebrew 'word for 'tent' (*'ohel*), with Oholah meaning 'her tent', and Oholibah, 'my tent in her'; that is, Oholibah refers to the sanctuary in Jerusalem, but this is not a satisfactory explanation. Some connection with 'tent' is most likely, and with that a suggestion of worship, but we cannot go beyond that.

Oholah was charged with faithlessness toward God because she
associated with *Assyrian lovers* (vv.5–8). Her punishment was to be
handed over to her *lovers* who destroyed her and her children
(vv.9–10). This refers to the historical situation of the fall of Samaria
and the exile of the people of the northern kingdom of Israel.

23.11–21 The main point of the story comes in the description of
what the younger sister, Oholibah, did. She saw what Oholah had
done but she did not learn from her sister's example. Rather, her
actions were much worse than those of her sister. (Although the
reference to the Assyrians is historically correct in that it refers to the
action of Judah in the time of Ahaz, II Kings 16.7–20, it is an addition
to the charges concerning the Babylonians, brought in from vv.5–6.)
She was attracted to the Babylonians by the *male figures carved on the
wall*, a sign of the power and military might of the Babylonians, and
sent messengers to them to come to her. She was defiled by her
relations with them. After this she turned from the Babylonians to
the Egyptians. In this Jerusalem was represented as going from one
alliance (lover) to another, which may refer to Zedekiah's appeal to
Egypt for help against the Babylonians who were besieging
Jerusalem (Jer.37; Ezek.17.11–18), or to the changes of policy which
took place between the death of Josiah and the fall of the city in 587
BCE. However, it is more likely that the prophet's condemnation was
directed generally against Israel's willingness to seek alliances when
threatened rather than put its trust in God (see Isa.7; 30; 31;
Hos.7.11–12; 12.1).

Judgement on the unfaithful one
23.22–27

Judgement on Oholibah would be executed by her *lovers*, as it was
for Oholah, her sister (v.22; compare with vv.9–10). In this instance
the Babylonians and their allies, coming as a strong invading force
and acting with the authority of God, would be the *lovers* to execute
judgement on the unfaithful sister (v.23). Their actions are described
in terms of the punishment of an adulteress, that is, stripping, muti-
lation, and killing children (vv.25–26). The city which had acted like
a harlot would be judged as a harlot (v.27) and her harlotry ended
(compare 16.35–43). *The Assyrians*, and the description of them, have
been added to v.23, as was required after the addition in v.12.

In presenting the charges and judgement against Jerusalem in this way Ezekiel drew on similar presentations in Hosea (2.2–13) and Jeremiah (3.6–11; 4.30). This not only reveals his knowledge of the earlier prophets, it also shows the way a prophet could take the words of a predecessor and re-present them for a new situation. In the case of the Hosea oracle, Ezekiel drew on words that had been fulfilled in the fall of Samaria, so giving his words added authority and a greater impact on the people.

Further judgement
   23.28–35

Three further statements of judgement have been added to vv.1–27. The first, vv.28–30, gives a summary of the judgement, brought by *those whom you hate* rather than the *lovers*, and an explanation of why the judgement would come on Jerusalem. It is more general than the judgement in vv.22–27, but it drew on that statement and on 16.7,39 in referring to the condition of Oholibah after those administering justice had finished with her. She would be *stark naked*, her condition as the foundling in ch.16.

23.31–34   The second addition is in the form of a poem on a cup of woe from which Oholibah had to drink, her sister's cup which signified ruin and desolation for Oholibah as it had for Oholah. The cup of woe or wrath is referred to a number of times in the Old Testament to signify God's judgement on the disobedient (e.g. Isa.51.17; Jer.25.15–29; 49.12–13; Pss.11.6; 75;8).

23.35   The third addition is an independent oracle of judgement which described Jerusalem's acts of 'harlotry' as *forsaking* God and restating that she must *bear the guilt* of her actions.

An appendix
   23.36–49

A further address has been added to vv.1–35, based on the earlier material, but developing it and applying it by drawing on chs.16 and 20. It differs from vv.1–35 in dealing with the sisters together rather than separately, and by including the charge of cultic apostasy (vv.36–39) with political apostasy (vv.40–44). The grammatical structure of the text, with a mixture of masculine and feminine, singular and plural and second and third person pronouns, indicates that this address is a collection of originally independent sayings which gave a further explanation of parts of vv.1–35.

23.36–39   The first addition charged the two sisters with cultic apostasy in the form of adultery with idols, child sacrifice (see 16.17,20–21,38), profaning the temple and desecrating the sabbath (see 20.16,21). This gave a more complete understanding of why Jerusalem had to be punished.

23.40–44   The second addition returns to the theme of political apostasy. It developed v.16 in conjunction with the imagery of ch.16 to show the enormity of Jerusalem's actions. The women sent messengers to bid men come to them from afar (see v.16), they prepared themselves lavishly to receive the men (see 16.9,11,13,18), and they committed adultery with them.

23.45–49   The third addition is a statement of judgement and is in two parts. In the first part judgement would be by upright men (v.45); that is, men who would decide correctly on those who were guilty of adultery and bloodshed (see v.37 and 16.38). In the second part judgement would be by the *mob*, a company of people brought together to execute judgement (see 16.40). This is described in terms very similar to 16.40–41, and the punishment for worship of alien gods in Deut.13.9–10. The conclusion in v.49 gives a summary of the reason for the judgement and the need to bear the penalty for idolatry (see vv.35,37,39;16.58).

These additions (vv.36–49) make it clear that God was correct in judging and punishing Samaria and Jerusalem, and that maintenance of the relationship with God required obedience.

The siege and capture of Jerusalem
24

Sayings on the cauldron
24.1–14

The date, January 588, and the command to record that date as the day the siege by the Babylonians began (vv.1–2), indicates that ch.24 relates to the siege and capture of Jerusalem.

There are two sayings about a cauldron. First there is an allegorical poem (*a song of derision*) about a *cauldron* filled with meat, *bones and water* to be cooked as a *stew* and then emptied out (vv.3–5,6b). In the similar saying in 11.3, the contents of the cauldron referred to the leaders of Jerusalem, but here it refers to the people of the city. In both cases the cauldron was the besieged city.

An interpretation of the allegory is given in vv.9–10, which makes it clear that God would be responsible for the cooking in the cauldron, making up the fire and making an end to the meat. That is, God was responsible for the siege and the destruction of the inhabitants in the city.

The second saying also likens Jerusalem to a cauldron (*pot*, vv.6b,11–12), but in this case it was corroded and could not be cleaned. Verse 7 makes it clear that the corrosion was the *blood* shed in the city and left uncovered on *bare rock*. Uncovered blood of a murder victim was said to cry out to God for vengeance (Gen.4.10; Job 16.18; Isa.26.21) so, by leaving shed blood lying on rock where it could not soak into the ground or be covered, Jerusalem showed disregard for God, and invited judgement. Further, God ensured that the spilt blood of the city was not covered, so that its call for vengeance would not be silenced but answered by God's judgement and punishment on the city (v.8). The only way to cleanse the cauldron was to heat it to such a point that the *corrosion* was *burnt off* (v.11). Similarly, the only way for Jerusalem to be cleansed was to have its people 'burnt off' in the fire of war (v.12).

24.13 and 14   are additions to stress that the corrosion could not be removed without the drastic action God had promised, and to identify the corrosion with lewdness which could only be removed by God's act of judgement against the people (see chs.16,20,23). Verse 14 emphasises that what was promised would come, for there would be no change of mind by God. The people would be judged according to their deeds (v.14).

The death of the prophet's wife
24.15–24

Ezekiel was instructed to perform a symbolic action which would convey an important message to the people at the time of the fall of Jerusalem. In this action he was instructed not to mourn, nor to show any *grief* when his *wife* suddenly *died*, and this he did (vv.16–18). It was a startling thing to do and inevitably caught the attention of the people. That he, a prophet, should do such a thing would immediately suggest to the people that an important event was about to happen which would have a marked effect on their lives. So, when the people asked the meaning of his action, they would not be surprised at the word of judgement Ezekiel spoke against them. They were about to lose the temple, the most precious sign of God's presence with them, and their children would die by the sword. When this happened they were not to mourn, but to do as Ezekiel had done, for he was a *sign* to Israel (v.24) and, like Jeremiah before him, he delivered the message that the calamity soon to befall Jerusalem was so great the people would be too numb to be involved in the usual mourning rites (Jer.16.5–9).

Implicit in Ezekiel's action and explanation is the thought that there was hope, just as there is hope for the living, even in the face of the death of those who are closest and most loved. The exiles were far from their land, but they were alive, and they had God's prophet with them, therefore there was hope.

News that the city had fallen
24.25–27

These verses form a 'bridge passage' between vv.15–24 and ch.33.21–22 which became necessary when the collection of prophecies against foreign nations was placed between the statement that the city would soon fall and the announcement that it had fallen. Verse 25 drew on v.21 which told of what God intended to do; that is, God would destroy the temple (*the stronghold whose beauty so gladdened them* [v.25] = *my sanctuary, which has been your strong boast* [v.21]), and take their children. Verses 26–27 drew on 33.21–22 where news of the fall of Jerusalem, which reached Ezekiel by means of a fugitive, cured his dumbness. Verses 26–27 prophesy the events of 33.21–22 with the suggested dumbness of the prophet providing the link between the two. The apparent disagreement between the two readings about when the event took place ('on that day', vv.25,26 [Hebrew text] and six months after the fall of the city, 33.21) is due to the way the two sources were combined. It is unlikely that the author intended to suggest that the fugitive arrived in Babylon on the day the city fell.

JUDGEMENT

The major thrust of the material in chs.4–24 is on judgement and punishment for Israel, the disobedient people of God. There are places where hope is offered, but this assumes the people will be judged and punished first. Such an emphasis may not be popular today but it points to an important element of faith in our relationship with God.

The assumption behind the catalogue of Israel's disobedience was that there existed a relationship between God and the people of Israel. This relationship began on God's initiative with the choice of Israel to be God's people, to whom God declared, 'I am the Lord your God', and whom God promised to 'bring out of Egypt into the land I had sought out for them' (Ezek.20.5–6). The woes, judgement and punishment were proclaimed therefore in the context of God's gracious action toward Israel.

A second feature of this context is the means God provided for Israel to be a faithful partner in the relationship. Israel was given God's statutes, ordinances and the sabbath 'that they might know that I the Lord sanctify them' (Ezek.20.11–12). That is, Israel was given the way to respond to God through obedience to the commandments God gave them. Failure to fulfil the commandments and observe the statutes and ordinances was to rebel against God and make Israel liable to the consequences of a broken relationship; that is, judgement and punishment (Deut. 28.15–63; Lev.26.18–39).

Ezekiel was called by God to proclaim that Israel had rebelled against God and to declare the consequences of rebellion for the people of Israel (Ezek.2.3–4). So he spoke of judgement in the form of God's decision to destroy Jerusalem and its people, and punishment in the form of death or exile to Babylon (e.g. Ezek.5.1–4, 5–12 ; 7.2–12; 15.1–5,6–8).

Yet within this doom and gloom Ezekiel held out the possibility that it would be different for Israel if the people renounced their sinful ways, kept the law and did what was just and right. If they would do that they would live and the offences committed would not be remembered against them (18.21–22; understanding the statement to apply to the people as well as an individual). The frequent statements of judgement and punishment were made to rouse the people to repentance. However, there was for Ezekiel, who was with the first group in exile and suffering punishment with his people, a strong sense that repentance would come only after the people had experienced judgement and punishment.

The situation for Israel in all of this is summed up in the question Ezekiel asked after the death of Pelatiah son of Benaiah (11.13), *Lord God, are you going to make an end of all the Israelites who are left?* That is, was this judgement and punishment the concluding act of God in the relationship with Israel? From the suggestions of hope which are found associated with some statements of judgement, it would appear that Ezekiel saw that there was hope and it lay in the survival and exile of some who would remember God (6.8–9; 20;43–44), who would have God's presence with them in exile and to whom God would give *singleness of heart ... and a new spirit* (11.16–20), with whom God would establish *a covenant which will last forever* (16.60–63) and return them to *the land which I swore to give your forefathers* (20.40–44).

So, the major points that are to be seen in relation to judgement in Ezekiel are:

1. Like all the experiences of Israel, judgement took place within the context of the relationship with God.

2. In the relationship Israel was called to respond to God's grace with obedience to God. The way of response was provided by God's laws, statutes and ordinances.

3. If Israel was not obedient, God's judgement would come upon the people as provided for in the lists of 'Blessings and Curses' at the conclusion of the accounts of the laws in Deuteronomy (ch.28) and Leviticus (ch.26).

4. Disobedience would result in judgement, although the people might answer God's call to turn from their disobedience, in which case God would forgive them.

5. But even in judgement God's part in the relationship would be maintained and God would forgive the people if they repented.

When we look at the book of Ezekiel as a whole, the emphasis on judgement makes a strong impression. Almost half the book is dominated by this theme (chs.2–24) from which Ezekiel is readily characterised as a prophet of doom. However, the latter part of the book turns to promise (chs.33–39) and restoration (chs.40–48). This structure fits the general chronology of that part of Israel's history: that is, statements of judgement before the loss of the kingdom and the land, words of promise when the people were experiencing punishment in exile, and a program of restoration when the people returned from exile and were settled again in their own land.

The question which often puzzles the modern reader is, Why does the book dwell so much on judgement and punishment when the writer knew of the hope that God would forgive the repentant people and provide for their resettlement in the land? One answer is that the consequences of our actions are real and are to be recognised as part of life. We of this century have ample evidence of this in our individual life and the experience of our communities. A straight 'cause and effect' explanation is too simple an answer for the personal tragedies which come to people, but we are aware of the part the consequences of our actions play in life. In many cases, when we view what has happened in a broad context, it is seen to be a major factor.

In our society we are reminded that corporate selfishness as well as individual greed is destructive of lives. For example, policies that deny the young opportunities for development and fulfilment risk high levels of hopelessness which have led to suicide and to violence in communities as people vent their frustration on an uncaring world. We cannot ignore this once we have read what is said in Ezekiel. These are the consequences of your actions, it says; see in them a judgement and turn away from those bad policies toward policies that bring life, hope and fulfilment.

Again, we see in Ezekiel a refusal to devalue judgement in the way in which God deals with people. Judgement is not just an incident on the way to forgiveness and renewal. It is not something to be quickly passed over as of little importance, rather it is an experience to be known and suffered in its reality. There is a strong sense that judgement must be lived with, even when there is the reality of hope and the expectation of renewal. As Ezekiel recognised, it speaks to us of the truth of God's care, that God, in the grace of the relationship with us, takes our participation in the relationship so seriously that we are judged, even as we are forgiven and renewed. To live with the God who judges is to live also with the God who gives hope in forgiveness and renewal.

In the New Testament judgement holds a central place in the message proclaimed. For example, Jesus declared its reality for all people which gave urgency to his call for repentance so that they might receive forgiveness (Matt.11.20–24; 13.24–30,40–43,47–50). It is only by God's grace that one may be forgiven and the assurance of that is through belief in Jesus (Matt.10.32–37; John 3.18–21). Jesus came to the world so that people might have life and be saved from judgement (John 3.17); that is, Jesus is the one who frees from the judgement of God because he is the one who brings the forgiveness of God.

Similarly, Paul looked to the righteous judgement of God to which all people are subject, but he did so in the confidence that the grace of God offered to all in Jesus Christ brings reconciliation and salvation for those who believe in Jesus (Rom.8.31–39).

The concept of judgement is basic to the traditions of the Christian faith. It does not negate the love of God which is also basic to our faith, rather, it gives the context within which the proclamation of God's love is made. All people come under the judgement of God, but God, in love through Jesus Christ, offers forgiveness and new life to those who will accept it.

This is not the end of the discussion. As has been foreshadowed, it continues in the presentation of hope for the people of Israel in exile in Babylon (chs.33–39) and then in the vision of those people restored to their homeland with a new temple and its renewed cult at the centre of the nation (chs.40–48).

Judgement against the nations
25–32

The book of Ezekiel moves from judgement on the people of Israel in chs.4–24 to judgement on foreign nations in chs.25–32. This central position for oracles against foreign nations is similar to other prophetic books of the Old Testament, especially Isaiah 1–39, and the Greek version of Jeremiah. (The English translations follow the Hebrew text of Jeremiah which has oracles against the nations near the end of the book.) In Ezekiel they come between words of judgement and punishment (chs.4–24) and words of hope, renewal, and reconstruction (chs.33–48).

The words of condemnation against the nations are presented in three main sections. First against Judah's neighbours, Ammon, Moab, Edom and Philistia; then Tyre (and Sidon); and finally Egypt. Each of these nations had dealings with Judah over the centuries leading up to the exile and were used by God in the judgement which came on Judah.

Against Israel's neighbours
25

Ammon
25.1–7

This is the first of four statements of judgement against Judah's neighbours, each of which was condemned for its attitude to Judah. The charge against Ammon is in two parts (vv.2–5 and vv. 6–7), each of which has the same form as the other statements in ch.24. that is, a report of what the nation did to Judah and God's judgement given as a consequence of that action. The second part (vv.6–7) is in general terms which reflect a time when the details of the fall and destruction of Ammon were no longer important to Israel. The description is similar to that used elsewhere in Ezekiel for the condemnation and

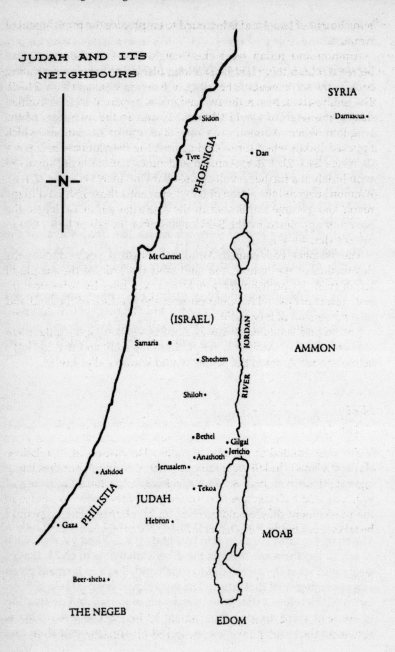

JUDAH AND ITS
NEIGHBOURS

SYRIA

Damascus •

Sidon •

—N—

Tyre •   • Dan

PHOENICIA

Mt Carmel •

(ISRAEL)

JORDAN

Samaria •

AMMON

• Shechem

RIVER

Shiloh •

• Bethel
              • Gilgal
         • Anathoth • Jericho

Jerusalem •

• Ashdod

• Tekoa

PHILISTIA

JUDAH

• Gaza

Hebron •

MOAB

Beer-sheba •

THE NEGEB

EDOM

punishment of Israel and is intended to emphasise the punishment of Ammon.

Ammon and Judah were close neighbours (see the map, p.80) between whom there had been a long history of antagonism dating back to the settlement of the tribes of Israel in Canaan (Num.21.24). The animosity between the two nations is apparent in their conflict during the reign of David (II Sam.10), and in the last years of the kingdom when Ammon was one of a group of nations which opposed Judah when it revolted against the Babylonians in 598 BCE (II Kings 24.1–2). Later, Ammon and other nations were involved with Judah in a further revolt against Babylon in 593 BCE (Jer.27.1–8). Ammon survived the action of Babylon against those involved in the revolt and became implicated in the assassination of Gedeliah, the governor appointed by the Babylonians after the fall of Jerusalem in 587 BCE (Jer. 40–41).

The prophet condemned Ammon because it rejoiced over the destruction of the temple, the land, and the exile of the people of Judah (v.3). Its punishment was to be taken over by *tribes from the east*, desert people who would plunder the produce of the land and take possession of it (vv.4–5).

The second statement (vv.6–7) emphasises that God's judgement was provoked by Ammon's delight in Judah's fall and that in God's action against Ammon the people would know God as Lord.

Moab

25.8–11

Moab was situated to the east of Judah. The history of its relationship with Israel/Judah was similar to that of Ammon, but the charge against Moab was that it did not acknowledge the uniqueness of Judah as God's chosen people. Ammon and Moab are linked also in the punishment they would receive; for Moab, like Ammon, would be taken over by *the tribes from the east* (v.10, compare v.4).

Edom

25.12–14

Edom was to the south-east of Judah. Although some relationship between Israel and Edom is seen in the identification of Esau, the brother of Jacob, as the ancestor of Edom (Gen.36.1), the history of their dealings with one another was one of antagonism and bitterness. The king of Edom prevented the Israelites from passing through his land as they journeyed toward Canaan after the exodus from Egypt (Num.20.14–21) and David is reported to have acted savagely against the Edomites when he slaughtered eighteen thousand of them and occupied their land (II Sam.8.13–14; I Kings 11.15–16).

Like Ammon and Moab, Edom was one of the nations which encouraged Judah to attempt to break free from Babylon in 593 BCE (Jer.27.1–8), but it escaped the destruction suffered by Judah and was able to occupy part of Judah's territory when Jerusalem fell to the Babylonians. Further evidence of antagonism is seen in the way Edom was roundly condemned by the prophets Isaiah, Jeremiah, Amos and Malachi (Isa.34.5–17; Jer.49.7–22; Amos 1.11–12; Mal.1.2–5).

Ezekiel charged Edom with taking *harsh revenge* on Judah, a reference to the occupation of the territory of Judah (v.15). The punishment would be the total destruction of Edom – *people, animals,* and *land* (v.13). A later writer has emphasised the antipathy between Judah and Edom by giving Judah (*my people Israel*) a direct part in bringing God's *vengeance* on Edom (v.14).

The Philistines
25.15–17

The Philistines arrived in the area from across the sea at about the time the Israelite tribes settled in Canaan following the exodus from Egypt and the wilderness wandering. They occupied an area on the coast to the west of Judah. The two groups were rivals for the land until David defeated the Philistines and secured the land for Israel (II Sam.5.17–25; 8.1). However, the Philistines continued to occupy the coastal area and animosity between the two neighbours remained to the time of the exile, as the words of the prophets show (Isa.14.28–32; Jer.47; Amos 1.6–8; Joel 3.4–8). The Philistines suffered at the hands of the Babylonians but, after the fall of Jerusalem, they were able to occupy some of the territory of Judah.

The charge against the Philistines, like that against Edom, was that they had revenged themselves against Judah *to satisfy an age-long enmity* (v.15). Their punishment was destruction, executed in God's *vengeance* and with *fury*.

As with the judgement against disobedient Israel, judgement on the neighbouring nations would be recognised as the action of God and the means by which God would be known as Lord by those who had rejoiced in Judah's fall and those who sought to profit from God's action against Judah (vv.5,7,11,17). In this action on behalf of Israel the faithfulness of God toward the covenant people would be revealed to the nations.

Against Tyre and Sidon
26–28

Tyre was a city to the north of Judah and was one of the main cities in the land of Phoenicia. It owed its fame to its location on an island just off the coast, which made it virtually impregnable, and its prominence as a centre for commerce and trade. Its reputation as a trading centre was dependant on the seagoing prowess of the Tyrians, the two good harbours on its island, and the fact that the Phoenicians occupied a narrow strip of land between the mountains and the coast. They were thus predisposed toward maritime trade.

Tyre, as a centre for commerce, was a source of influence on Israel and Judah. Solomon engaged Hiram from Tyre to be in charge of the building of the temple (I Kings 7.13–14). Later the fertility cult of the Tyrian Baal was fostered in Israel as a result of the marriage of Jezebel, a Tyrian princess, to Ahab, king of Israel (I Kings 16.29–33). This cult was a constant cause of apostasy by the people of Israel and Judah and was vigorously opposed and condemned by the prophets (e.g. Hos.4; Jer.2–3; Ezek.16; 23). Ezekiel's strong condemnation of Tyre came from his attitude toward the alien cults in Judah. He was vehemently opposed to the city which was the centre of the pernicious fertility cult, especially as Tyre was one of the 'nations' which encouraged Judah to revolt against the Babylonians in 593 BCE.

After the fall of Jerusalem, Nebuchadrezzar began a long siege of Tyre. Ezekiel's words are from that period: four statements of judgement similar to those against Judah's neighbours in ch. 25, a lament over Tyre (ch.26), the ship that had sunk (ch.27), judgement on the king of Tyre (28.1–10) and a lament over him (28.11–19).

Judgement against Tyre
26.1–21

The four judgement statements against Tyre in ch.26 are introduced with the date on which God spoke to the prophet (v.1). The month of the year is missing from the Hebrew text of 26.1 and has been supplied from the Greek text in the REB. The *first month* of the REB is almost certainly too early as the statements assume the fall of Jerusalem which was later in the year.

Judgement for the spite of Tyre (26.2–6)

The first word of judgement (vv.2–6) came as a result of Tyre rejoicing over the fall of Jerusalem and its anticipation of the advantage Jerusalem's demise would be to Tyre (v.2). In response, the prophet pronounced God's punishment in terms that drew on the island location of the city. The imagery of *many nations* raised up against the city like *waves* raised by the sea (v.3) heightens the sense of the destruction that would come to Tyre as it is taken up in v.4. Also, the picture of an island, so bare that it may be used to dry nets, emphasises that Tyre would be utterly destroyed, along with the Phoenician coastal cities *her daughters on the mainland* (vv.5–6).

Destruction of Tyre by Nebuchadrezzar (26.7–14)

The three remaining statements of judgement in ch.26 are presented without introductory reasons for the action and so differ from the first statement. However, the reason given in v.2 may be seen to apply to all the words of judgement in the chapter. The second statement (vv.7–14) is similar to the first, but it is longer and has more detail, giving it the appearance of an expanded version of the first statement. The description begins by specifically referring to Nebuchadrezzar as the great and powerful king who would lead the mighty forces of destruction against Tyre (v.7) and appears to be a reference to the thirteen-year siege of Tyre by the Babylonians begun in 585 BCE. Description of how the action against Tyre would proceed follows: destruction of the coastal cities and erection of the siege-works against Tyre (vv.8–9), entry of the horsemen and their destruction of the city (vv.10–11), the loss of wealth and culture, reduction of the city to rubble and the island to a *bare rock, a place where nets are spread to dry* (vv.12–14). Verses 13–14 draw on vv.4–5a to heighten the picture of total destruction which God would bring against Tyre, the city *never* to *be rebuilt* (v.14).

Fear and lament at the destruction of Tyre (26.15–18)

The third judgement is in the form of a report of how the destruction of Tyre would be received by its neighbours and trading partners and the lament that would be raised. A funeral lament (vv.17–18), which is similar to 27.32–36, is preceded by descriptions of the fear and mourning of those who would see the destruction of Tyre (vv.15–16). Shaking by the *coasts and islands* recognises the fear they would feel that such terror and destruction may come to them, and the actions of the *sea-kings* are the mourning rites which would be followed by the rulers of the peoples with whom Tyre traded. Their lament recognises the renown and influence of Tyre which would be ended, to their dismay.

Tyre's descent to the abyss (26.19–21)

The last judgement statement has connections with 32.17–32, from which it applies to the destruction of Tyre the image of descent into the abyss, the underworld place for the dead. This then would be the end for Tyre. It would not be seen again in the *land of the living* (vv.20–21).

A lament over Tyre
27.1–36

A lament (REB 'dirge') in two parts (vv.3b–11, 25b–36), separated by a prose section (vv.12–24), carries on the judgement against Tyre. The status of Tyre as an important sea trader with a prominent location for that trade is recognised in the introduction to the lament (v.3a).

A lament for the lost ship of Tyre (27.3b–11, 25–36)

The lament begins by depicting Tyre as a ship built to sail the seas. Most scholars accept that the first line of the lament should read 'Tyre, you are a ship of perfect beauty', the present reading being the result of a scribal error. The ship was made of the best materials available to a maritime power; a thing of beauty, crewed by the best in their trade drawn from the neighbouring cities (vv.3b–9a).

27.9b–11 The picture changes from a ship to the city. The harbour of the city attracted the ships of many traders. Such was the wealth and power of Tyre that it was able to hire mercenaries for its defence, people drawn from locations spread round the eastern end of the Mediterranean Sea.

27.25b–36 The lament returns to the picture of a ship. This suggests that vv.9b–11 were added at a later time to emphasise the strength of Tyre and, as in vv.8–9a, to show that Tyre could draw people from a wide area to serve it.The lament envisages the ship fully laden and taken out to the high sea (*many waters*) where it was wrecked by an east wind, a total loss (vv.25b–27). All who sailed the sea mourned the wreck and its loss with signs of grieving (vv.29–31), and raised a lament (vv.32–36). There is thus a lament within a lament which describes the former glory of Tyre and its present distress. It was incomparable, now it is gone, with all its glory, splendour and power (vv.32b–34). All who saw its fall were deeply shocked at its fate (v.35).

Tyre's many partners (27.12–24)

The major addition which separates the two parts of the lament (vv.12–25a) is a list of the names of nations with whom Tyre traded, nations from all round the Mediterranean area and extending to Mesopotamia in the east. The purpose of the list was to show what an important trading power Tyre was at that time. Nations are referred to as either *the source* of goods (for example, Tarshish, v.12,Edom, v.16, Damascus, v.18) or having *offered* things to Tyre (for example, Togarmah, v.14, Judah and Israel, v.17). The structure of the list shows that Tyre conducted trade in such a way that the nations were dependant on it and its loss would be a cause for mourning to all the trading partners.

27.36 The last verse of the lament is almost the same as 28.19 and introduces an element of derision against Tyre and the declaration that it would *be no more* (v.36). This is an addition made to emphasise that Tyre's end was complete and it would not be mourned by all people. That is, it puts the position of Judah, which would rejoice at the downfall of its powerful neighbour which had sought to profit from Judah's destruction (26.2). It also leads in to the judgement and lament of Tyre's rulers in ch.28.

Against the rulers of Tyre
28.1–19

The lament for Tyre is followed by a message of judgement against its ruler ('prince', vv.1–10) and a lament over him (*king*, vv.11–19). Apart from indicating that they had different origins, there does not appear to be any significance in the use of different terms for ruler in the two parts of the passage. It was rulers as a whole, and as representatives of their people, rather than a particular ruler who was judged in vv.1–19.

Against the prince of Tyre (28.1–10)

The form of the judgement in vv.1–10 is similar to the statements against the nations in ch.25, beginning with the reason for judgement (vv.2–5) and proceeding to words of judgement (vv.6–10). The charge is that the *ruler*, in his *arrogance*, thought of himself as a god and *enthroned like a god*. It was accepted in some ancient eastern cultures that the king was a god, but such a thought was right outside Israelite belief, as *you are a man and no god* shows (v.2). An addition to the text accepts that the ruler was wise, and that his wisdom had gained him wealth and extensive trade, but that did not make him a god (vv.3–5).

The consequence of the ruler's opinion of himself was that God would bring judgement upon him. Nations would attack and destroy him, confirming that he was not a god (vv.6–10). The purpose of this judgement against Tyre is shown in the concluding formula, *I have spoken. This is the word of the Lord God* (v.10). The God of Israel could cause judgement to fall on Tyre and its ruler, and when this happened, God's power and position as God would be confirmed and the proud claim of the ruler of Tyre would be shown to be false.

A lament for the ruler of Tyre (28.11–19)

Verses 11–19 are a lament over the *king of Tyre* in which the king is likened to the first man who lived in Eden until iniquity caused his downfall and expulsion. The original lament has been expanded to highlight the king's position and splendour, and to relate his downfall to the judgement given in vv.1–10. This presents some difficulties in the text, but the sense of the lament is generally clear.

28.12–14   The first part of the lament establishes the king's position and glory, he was the sign of perfection and full of wisdom and beauty. He dwelt in the garden of Eden but, in contrast to Adam who was naked, he wore clothes decorated with precious stones and gold. The list of precious stones (v.13) draws on the list given in the description of the high priest's breast-plate in Exod.28.17–20, which suggests some priestly connection for the king who was *on God's holy mountain* (v.14). *Stones of fire* completes the picture of splendour, symbolising either sparkling jewels or the stars among which the gods of some mythologies were said to walk.

28.15–17   The second part of the lament continues the imagery of paradise and fall to describe the king's ruin because of his iniquity (v.15). His iniquity was attributed to his commerce, because it led to lawlessness and banishment from his exalted position, and his beauty, which led to arrogance. The king's misuse of wisdom to enhance splendour resulted in his being debased in the sight of the kings.

28.18–19   Desecration of sanctuaries through trading has been added to the iniquities of which the king was guilty. For this he was destroyed by fire within, a reference to the destruction of the city of Tyre. Tyre would be *no more*, much to the dismay of the nations.

Against Sidon
28.20–23

The final judgement on Judah's neighbours is against Sidon, a Phoenician city on the Mediterranean coast to the north of Tyre. There is no reference to any action of Sidon to justify the judgement and destruction proclaimed against the city (vv.22–23). It was involved with the nations which conspired with Judah to break free from Babylon in 593 BCE (Jer.27.1–8), but this is not mentioned. Rather, the reason for the action against Sidon was that God would be glorified (v.22) and known among the people (vv.22, 23). The terms which describe the destruction are similar to those found elsewhere in Ezekiel to signify utter destruction (v.23).

This saying against Sidon has the appearance of an addendum placed here to complete the cycle of judgement sayings against Judah's neighbours.

Concluding remarks
28.24–26

28.24 The first conclusion follows vv.20–23, but it relates to the whole collection of sayings in chs.25–28. The outcome of God's judgement on Judah's neighbours (the *briars* and *thorns*) would be peace for *the Israelites* and for God to be known as God.

28.25–26 A second conclusion looks forward to the return of the exiles to dwell securely in their own land, but it could not happen until God's judgement was executed on Judah's *scornful neighbours*. The cycle of sayings has been provided with a hopeful conclusion.

Against Egypt
29–32

There are seven statements against Egypt to conclude Ezekiel's oracles against foreign nations. All but the third (30.1–19) are dated and all the dates except the second belong to the period of the siege of Jerusalem, its fall to Nebuchadrezzar and the time immediately after its fall; that is, January 588 to March–April 586 (or 585) BCE; see below on 32.1,17. The exception (29.17) is the latest date in the book of Ezekiel.

Egypt had a long association with Israel and was an important influence in the nation's life. It was to Egypt's advantage to control the area occupied by Israel because it was the way that had to be taken if there were to be any military or trade dealings between Egypt and the nations to the north east. Israel was therefore a good buffer zone to protect Egypt from the great powers which rose in the Mesopotamian region, and it provided a route for the rich trade between the African continent and Asia.

Egypt was involved in the unstable political situation which characterised Judah's life from the death of Josiah to the fall of Jerusalem. Josiah was killed by the Egyptians in 609 BCE when he unsuccessfully attempted to prevent them marching north to do battle with the Babylonians (II Chron.35.20–24). The Egyptians were defeated by the Babylonians in the ensuing battle and, on their return through Judah they deposed Jehoahaz, whom the people of Judah had made king in Josiah's stead, and placed Jehoiakim on the throne in his place (II Kings 23.31–35). The Babylonians defeated the Egyptians again in 605 and took control of the area to the south of Judah. In the face of this threat Jehoiakim transferred his allegiance to the Babylonians and Judah remained under Babylonian control until the revolt in 588 BCE.

During this time Egypt, as a possible source of help against the Babylonians, remained a disturbing influence for Judah. In 588 Judah revolted with support from Egypt. The Babylonians reacted swiftly by putting Jerusalem under siege (II Kings 25.1–2; Jer.37.5). The Egyptian army marched towards Jerusalem which caused the Babylonians to raise the siege to go to fight them (Jer.37.5). The Babylonians defeated the Egyptians and returned to re-apply the siege. They took the city in 587 BCE, destroyed it and the temple, and exiled many of the inhabitants to Babylon (II Kings 25.4; Jer.39.2). Some of the people of Judah fled to Egypt during the exilic period (Jer. 42.14–22; 43).

Judgement on Pharaoh and the land
29.1–16

This is the earliest statement about Egypt, dated at the beginning of 587 BCE (v.1), which was during the siege of Jerusalem, a few months before the fall of the city. It consists of four parts which have been brought together to form a declaration of judgement against Pharaoh and Egypt.

29.2–6a The introduction, with its command to *face towards* and *prophesy against* (v.2), shows that what was to be said was against Pharaoh, a point that is made by the opening words of the oracle (v.3). God was against Pharaoh, who was like a sea monster lying in the Nile, which he claimed to have created. Mention of the *great monster* suggests the crocodiles which inhabited the Nile, but it also suggests the monsters which were seen as beings in whom were concentrated the powers opposed to God in creation (Ps.74.13–14). The judgement which follows came because of the pride of Pharaoh, who claimed to have created the Nile, and to own it (v.3). Because of this he would be dragged from the stream to be eaten by beasts and birds and allowed to rot. Thus he would be dishonoured in death and, because he would not be buried properly, denied an after life.

God would then be known by Egypt as Lord to whom its Pharaoh and people were subject (vv.4–6a).

29.6b–9a A second judgement of destruction by the sword and desolation for the land was pronounced (vv.8–9a) because Egypt had appeared to support the Israelites, but that support did not eventuate when it was needed (vv.6b–7). The imagery of the reed that splintered or broke when used for support is particularly graphic in telling of an unreliable ally.

29.9b–12 The third judgement takes up Pharaoh's presumptuous claim to have created the Nile (v.3). Because of this Egypt would be destroyed and made desolate *from Migdol* in the north-east *to Syene* in the far south, that is, the whole land. It would lie desolate for forty years and its people be scattered among the nations, a punishment it would share with Judah (see 4.6 and 12.15; 22.15).

29.13-16 The statement as a whole closes with an assurance that at the end of forty years Egypt, like Judah, would be restored and its people brought back to their land of origin, the southern part of Egypt (vv.13–14). Egypt would not become a great nation again, but exist as a petty kingdom (vv.14–15) which would not tempt Israel to look to it for support (v.16). There is, however, an indication that God's purpose was not only to destroy those who in pride declared themselves outside the divine creative power, it also was to bring justice and to lead those who have been punished back to their place in God's scheme of things.

Recompense for Nebuchadrezzar
29.17–21

This is the latest dated passage in Ezekiel, March/April 571 BCE. It is therefore later than the lifting of the thirteen-year siege of Tyre by Nebuchadrezzar. The plundering and destruction of that city expected by Ezekiel (see on 26.7–14) had not occurred, so the reward anticipated by the investing army was not realised. The prophet appears to have believed that Nebuchadrezzar, who acted as the instrument of God, deserved some compensation, and this would take the form of Egypt which God would give to him to despoil and plunder (vv.19–20). Egypt's attitude to God in denying God's authority was a further reason for God's action (vv.20). That is, Egypt would be judged and punished through the same action which brought reward to Nebuchadrezzar.

The last verse (v.21) is an addition to vv.17–20. It is a word of promise that when Egypt was given to Nebuchadrezzar, new strength (lit. 'to make a horn sprout') would come to Israel and the prophet would regain his power *to speak among them*. This differs from other places where Ezekiel is said to receive back the power of speech (3.27; 24.27; 33.22). In those instances it is stated that the prophet had been dumb and the return of the power of speech overcame the dumbness. There is no reference to the prophet having been dumb in v.21 which suggests that at the time of Egypt's defeat he would speak with the confidence of one whose words had been vindicated.

The day of the Lord for Egypt
  30.1–19

As with the other statements against Egypt, the prophet was commanded to speak, but there is no date associated with this statement. It could have come from any time in the period between the first and last dates attached to the oracles against foreign nations; that is from 587 to 571 BCE.

30.2–4,6   A poem which proclaims the *day of the Lord* for Egypt begins the statement. The day would be a day of judgement and devastation for Egypt as the prophet had seen it would be for Judah (7.5–14). The whole of Egypt would be destroyed (vv.3–4), along with all who supported her (v.6). *Anguish in Cush* recognises the close relationship between Egypt and Cush (Ethiopia) so that suffering in Egypt would be felt in Ethiopia through threat of invasion or loss of trade and protection. (Verse 5 has been added to identify others who supported Egypt and who could expect to suffer along with Egypt.)

30.7–8   The poem has been further developed in terms of other prophetic material. Verse 7 draws on 29.12 to emphasise that destruction of Egypt and its helpers would be complete. It also employs a duplication of terms which is characteristic of the book of Ezekiel, *most desolate of desolate lands … most derelict of derelict cities*. Terms similar to Amos 1.4 are used to refer to the destruction of foreign nations, the action by which God would be known (acknowledged) as Lord.

30.9   Another expansion which comments on the *anguish in Cush* (v.4) by the application of the saying about messengers sent by ship from Cush to Jerusalem in Isa.18. In this verse the direction of travel has been reversed; the messengers would go from God's presence to Cush, and they would be the cause of the anguish, for their journey and their message would be associated with the destruction of Egypt whose hour was near.

30.10–12   A second poem, which drew on ch.29, deals with the way destruction would come to Egypt. It would come by the hand of Nebuchadrezzar who, at the instigation of God, would destroy the land by the sword (29.17–21), and by drought caused by God who would dry up the Nile (compare 29.9–12). In both cases the destruction would be the action of God.

30.13–19   The final poem reiterates that the whole of Egypt would be destroyed by listing the cities of its land and what their fate would be. It speaks of judgement, wrath and destruction. Although most of these cities were to be found in the Nile delta region, the intention was to emphasise that all of Egypt would be destroyed in the judgement of God.

The main point of the statement is that the judgement and destruction which would fall on Egypt would be the work of God who was the one who had power in history. It proclaims that the God of the people Israel had power over the nations and the works of God could be seen in the destiny of those nations. In this the people would *know that I* (God) *am the Lord* (v.19). For a people who languished in exile and whose only hope was in their God this was an important message which confirmed their hope and pointed to a future for them.

Pharaoh's broken arms

30.20–26

Two statements with the common theme of breaking Pharaoh's arms have been brought together in this short section. The passage is dated, April 587, which is three months after the first statement about Egypt (29.1), and three months before the fall of Jerusalem.

The first statement says that God had broken Pharaoh's arm which, because the break would not be treated, would make Pharaoh weak and unable to defend himself (v.21). This refers to Nebuchadrezzar's defeat of the Egyptian forces which had gone to the aid of besieged Jerusalem (Jer.37.5–10). Not only was that hoped for deliverance destroyed, but any further hope in Egypt was shown to be futile. Judah was therefore warned against the temptation to trust in foreign powers, a warning which was important also for the exilic and post-exilic communities.

30.22–26   The second statement concerns the fall of Egypt at the hands of Nebuchadrezzar. It is a threat against Egypt, the foreign nation, rather than a warning to Judah that it should not trust foreign powers (compare v.21, above), and has been joined to the first statement with the addition of *both his arms, the sound and the broken* (v.22) to accommodate the differences between the two. Pharaoh was to be rendered helpless with two broken arms and therefore would be unable to hold a sword (v.22), while the king of Babylon's arms would be strengthened by God, who would put *my sword* in his hand (v.24). Egypt's inability to resist Babylon is shown by *he will lie wounded and groaning before him* (v.24).

Two further additions, using the same words in each, have been made in vv.23 and 26. They extend the result of Egypt's defeat by Babylon to scattering and dispersing the Egyptians among the nations. This is similar to 29.12. The words are clearly an addition in v.23, where they inappropriately break in to the account of the defeat of Egypt, and in v.26, where they are included to 'round off' the statement against Egypt. Verse 25, which repeats what is said in v.24, is also an addition. It emphasises that God was responsible for what would happen to Egypt, for God gave strength to the arms of Nebuchadrezzar and put the sword in his hand to destroy Egypt.

A great tree falls
   31.1–18

Chapter 31 consists of a poem (vv.3–9) with a suitable introduction (vv.1–2) and two interpretations (vv.10–14 and 15–18). The chapter is introduced with the date of the saying, June 587, near the end of the siege of Jerusalem, and a command to the prophet to speak to *Pharaoh and his hordes* (vv.1–2a). *Hordes* refers not only to the many people in Egypt, it also refers to the pomp or glory of Pharaoh. It thus leads in to the question, *In your greatness, what are you like?* (v.2b), and is picked up again in the concluding judgement on *Pharaoh and all his hordes* (glory) (v.18).

The answer to the question of v.2b is given in the poem, vv. 3–9, and the interpretation, vv.10–14. The poem begins with what is thought by most scholars to be an error in the text. 'Assyria' is clearly out of place in this context. It occurs in a series of sayings against Egypt, and it is not referred to anywhere else in ch.31 to make a parallel or a contrast with Egypt. The name of a type of tree, with spelling similar to Assyria, must have stood at that place in the text. In a similar occurrence in 27.6 an emended form of the word gives cypress, which is probably the word intended here. The phrase, *it was a cedar of Lebanon*, is then to be seen as an addition to explain 'Assyria' in the context of the poem.

The poem was almost certainly an independent piece of material available to the prophet which he used to make a statement against Egypt. It reflects beliefs of the time about the structure of the world with a great cosmic tree at the centre of the earth which reached to the heavens and sent its roots to the waters below the earth. The tree gave shelter for animals and human beings, and in its branches birds nested (v.6). It was the most splendid of the trees in God's garden, and the envy of other trees (v.9).

31.10–14   The poem is interpreted in terms of judgement on Egypt. The cause of the judgement was Egypt's pride, which increased as the tree (Pharaoh) grew. God gave the tree to the *prince of the nations* (Nebuchadrezzar) to deal with (v.11), to *the most ruthless of nations* (the Babylonians) to cut it down and to spread it over mountains, valleys and water channels; that is, everywhere. No longer would it be a place of shelter (vv.12–13). Two further comments warn other leaders of the danger of pride (v.14a) and remind them that they are all mortal and destined for the underworld (*abyss*, v.14b).

31.15–18   A second interpretation carries on the thought of the underworld (Sheol) from v.14b. The tree would not only fall, it would go down to Sheol the place of the dead, the waters of the deep would be stopped in grief, Lebanon and all the trees would be affected (v.15). The nations would shake because of their fear at what had happened and all the trees (the leaders of the nations) would go down to Sheol, where they would draw comfort from the great tree being there (vv.16–17). Judgement against Egypt was thus the judgement which had and would come to all the nations, even one led by such a splendid leader as Pharaoh.

The last verse goes back to the question raised in v.2a, but it has been re-written to ask, *which among the trees of Eden was like you in glory and greatness?* The response is to be understood as 'none', but it would still end in the world below as would they, for all would be judged and end in shame and ignominy. This would be the fate of *Pharaoh and his hordes* (v.18).

A dirge over Pharaoh
  32.1–16

This section is introduced as a 'dirge' that the prophet was commanded to raise over Pharaoh king of Egypt (v.2a). The dirge form, however, is found only in v.2b, which is part of a dirge delivered by the prophet. The remainder of the section consists of a statement of judgement (vv.3–8), to which additions concerning the fall of Egypt and the consequences of that fall have been made (vv.9–15), and a concluding comment about the dirge (v.16).

The date of the command to the prophet, March 585 BCE (v.1), is later than that given in the next section, which is April 586 BCE. Other manuscripts read 'eleventh year' instead of *twelfth year*, giving March 586 in v.1. This may be the correct date, but it is possible that these two final sections have been interchanged to emphasise the end of Egypt as it is presented in vv.17–32.

32.2   Pharaoh is likened in the dirge first to a *young lion*, making reference to his vigour and stature among the nations (particularly appropriate if it were to be seen as a reference to the young and vigorous Hophra, but we cannot be sure about this), whose *end has come*, and then to a *monster in the seas*. REB has *in the waters of the Nile*, but the image here is of a monster in the primeval waters of chaos, not of a crocodile type creature as in 29.3. The opposition between God and the proud, defiant Pharaoh is made clear by likening Pharaoh to the monster which ruled the deep. Although the metaphor is changed, it is the end of Pharaoh, lion and/or sea monster, that is lamented.

32.3–8   Here judgement is given which uses the image of the sea monster to portray the end of Pharaoh in cosmic terms similar to chs.29.5 and 31.12–13. It speaks of making a complete end with humiliating destruction, as shown by *fling you on the land, dash you to the ground,* and leaving the carcass to be eaten by *birds* and *wild beasts* on *mountains* and *valleys* (vv.4–6). This judgement would be accompanied by *darkness* which may recall the plague of darkness with which God afflicted Egypt when Pharaoh refused to release the Israelite slaves to Moses (Exod.10.21–23). It is also similar to the visions of the end in Joel 2.2,10; 3.15. The end of the monster (Pharaoh) would be complete.

32.9–10   The image of the monster has not been carried on into this addition. Rather, it deals with the effect of the fall of Egypt on the nations round about it. They would view it with horror and with fear for their own positions.

32.11–14   This further addition has taken up *sword* (v.10) as a catch-word to designate Nebuchadrezzar as the instrument by which God would destroy Egypt, as in 29.19–20 and 30.24. It also takes up the churning of the waters from v.2, now with the sense of desolation, for the waters of the Nile would be disturbed no longer by men or cattle (*foot or hoof*), they would be removed from the land. The waters would become smooth, a sign that God's action against Egypt was complete.

God's action in destroying Egypt is further attested in v.15, a conclusion added to vv.3–14 to accentuate the point made in those verses; that is, destruction of this proud land would be seen as an action in which God was revealed.

32.16   The passage as a whole concludes with an identification of all that has gone before as a *dirge*. As noted above, this is a free use of the term as the material includes little that conforms to the form of 'dirge' or 'lament' found elsewhere in biblical literature. It calls on mourners to lament the end of Egypt and so emphasises the importance of this event.

Egypt's descent to the underworld
   32.17–32

The last saying against Egypt is dated in 586 BCE, after the fall of Jerusalem. (The *first month*, April, is absent from the Hebrew and has been taken from the Greek text.) It threatens Egypt with an ignoble end in the underworld.

There are difficulties in the text of this section and a number of suggestions have been made to arrive at a text that makes sense. Some of these suggestions have been adopted by REB.

The prophet was commanded to *raise a lament* over *the hordes* ('pomp', see above on 31.2) *of Egypt*. From what follows it is clear that this is different from the 'dirge' found in ch.31 and other places in Ezekiel and the Hebrew Bible. It lacks the characteristic rhythm of the 'dirge' (as for example, in 19.1–9) and appears to be a type of song of sorrow over the fate of a person or nation, in this case over Egypt, which would be consigned by God to the underworld (v.18).

A question, *Are you better favoured than others?* (v.19a; literally, To whom are you more lovely?), which recalls the beginning of the poem of the great tree in ch.31, begins the lament. As in ch.31, the intention was to show that Egypt was not superior to the other nations. This is seen clearly in vv.19b, 20b, which assigned Egypt and its allies a place with 'the uncircumcised dead' and 'those slain by the sword', phrases which described those who died without honour, either because they died in infancy before they could be circumcised and therefore could not be buried with the circumcised, or those who suffered a violent death.

The remainder of v.20 and all of v.21 are made up of additions to the text, partly by way of explanation, and partly through summary and reflection on the lament that follows. The result is a complicated passage which does not add anything to the understanding of the lament.

32.22–26   The lament is taken up again in v.22 and cites the situations of three powerful nations of the past, Assyria (vv.22–23), Elam (vv.24–25), and Meshech (and) Tubal (vv.26–27, see below), all of whom, with their people, were in the underworld. Each one is condemned by the description of its place in the underworld. Assyria, a great power which had much influence on the people of Israel until its final defeat at Nineveh in 612 BCE, was among the *victims of the sword* and in the place of greatest dishonour, *the farthest depths of the abyss.*

Elam, a nation to the east of Babylon, had been defeated by Assyria in 650 BCE and ceased to be a major force from that time. Its people were *victims of the sword* and bearing *disgrace with those who go down to the abyss* (v.24). There is much repetition in vv.24–25 which suggests that additions have been made to the text. The Greek text omits all of v.25 except *in the midst of the slain.* Also, *They have gone down uncircumcised to the world below* may be an addition in v.24. The grammatical structure is unusual and the use of *uncircumcised* in a non-technical sense is out of place in the context.

Meshech and Tubal were nations in Asia Minor which had been powerful enough to threaten Assyria in the seventh century. The Hebrew text treats them as one by omitting the conjunction 'and' (supplied from the Greek in REB), and by using singular pronominal suffixes in referring to the people of the two nations; that is, *its hordes buried about it.* These nations and their people are described as *uncircumcised, slain by the sword*, people who had *once spread terror in the land of the living*, which explained why they were in the depths of the underworld.

32.27   There are difficulties with this verse, which REB seeks to overcome by translating the text as a question rather than a sentence, so that it is consistent with v.26 and refers to Meshech/Tubal. However, it should be seen as a statement which contrasts the fate of those who died in dishonour (vv.22–26) with that of those who died as heroes (v.27b). This is made clearer with a minor emendation to the text, as suggested from the Greek, to give *They do not rest with warriors, the fallen from of old.* The description that follows is of the burial of those who had fallen with honour in battle, which emphasises the dishonour of the three great nations which rest in the abyss, far from the place of those who had fallen in honour.

32.28   The lament concludes with a direct address to Egypt, which, with its hordes, would lie in the company of those who died in dishonour. *Pharaoh* of REB is not in the Hebrew text and it is inappropriate as the lament is addressed to *Egypt's hordes* (v.18).

32.29–30   Additions have been made to the lament to include Edom, *all the princes of the north* and *the Sidonians*, Judah's neighbours, who were or had been her enemies. Edom and Sidon were dealt with earlier (25.12–14 and 28.20–23). The reference to *the Sidonians* suggests that the Phoenicians are intended here, but this may be an explanation of *all the princes of the north.*

32.31–32   contain further additions. The first is God's declaration that Pharaoh's comfort would be in his recognition that the situation of Egypt and its hordes was shared by other great nations of the past (v.31). The second affirms that, although Pharaoh and others may have appeared to be in control of what they did to terrorise Israel, they were acting as God allowed them (v.32). The Hebrew makes this clear by using the first person, 'For I have set his *terror* in the *land of the living.'*

This last addition affirms that the purpose of the oracles against foreign nations was to assure the exiles that the nations were under God's control and that, although Israel had been defeated and carried off into exile, God had not been defeated by the gods of the nations. At the appropriate time, God would defeat the nations and their gods and punish those who had acted against God's people. They would be unable to prevent Israel's restoration by God, nor would they be able to prevent God caring for Israel when the people were restored and resettled in the land. These oracles have an important place in the overall plan of the book of Ezekiel as it points to a future hope for the people of Israel.

ORACLES AGAINST THE NATIONS

These statements of judgement against the nations originate from the time of the fall of Jerusalem and soon after. The dates given at the beginning of some statements, and references to the attitudes of the nations to Israel, show this. In this context we see three things about God's dealing with people.

First, they show God dealing with things as they were for Israel. Exile in Babylon was not the only experience for Israel at the time. They had been subject also to harsh treatment by their near neighbours and by Egypt and Tyre. Indeed, each of the nations judged had contributed in some way to the present state of Israel and had an interest in having things remain as they were. Ezekiel recognises this, both in terms of how the nations felt towards Israel and towards God, and points to what God would do about it. In doing this he gave Israel confidence that their return to their own land would not be impeded by the nations that had previously opposed them.

Second, they make a statement about the power and extent of the influence of the God of Israel. God's threatened actions against Jerusalem had been fulfilled when the threats were made against the nations. Now the prophet speaks against the nations to proclaim the power of Israel's God over them. They had afflicted Israel and attempted to exalt themselves at the expense of God, but God's judgement would come on them as it had come on Israel. The God of Israel was God over the nations and, as it was said of Israel when God acted against it, so by God's actions against the nations *they will know that I am the Lord* (e.g. 25.17; compare e.g. 6.10,14).

This was Israel's assurance. Because God was God over the nations, they could not prevent God acting to save Israel. It may be compared with the great statements of Second Isaiah who, by recalling God's power in creation, gave confidence in God's power to act for the exiles (see e.g. Isa. 40.21–31; 43.1–15; 45.7–12).

These two things are important for people of faith today. The Bible consistently points to God's dealing with people in their life situations. In the Old Testament it is seen in the account of a slave people released by the action of God, the wandering of a people without a homeland, settlement in the land they had been promised and the struggles that involved, and then making a life in a hostile environment of constant threat from their neighbours. In all this God was involved with the people in day-to-day decisions, in joys, in sorrow and pain, in judgement, punishment, forgiveness and restoration. God was with them in every situation, whatever the situation. When they were tempted to forget that, God's prophets, such as Isaiah, Jeremiah and Ezekiel, recalled for them the way God had been with them and was now with them.

The life of Jesus, lived among the ordinary people of the day, speaks loudest of God's desire to be involved in the life situations of people. He lived with people and for people, caring for them and pointing to the way of God in their present experience of life. God's commitment to being with us in our living is shown also in Christ's handing on his work to those who followed him and by giving the Holy Spirit that we may be guided and sustained in life.

Today God deals with us in our life situations through the blessing of continuing provision of all that we need in life, the care of those who are concerned for the well-being of all God's people in justice and peace, and the leadership of those who seek to bring us nearer to God in response to all that God is. When this is done in the spirit of God in Christ, it does not take us out of life with all its demands but confirms for us the truth that life is a blessing which God bestows and which God enables us to live. Even though we may feel as though we are in exile and all about us is against us, God is with us in the struggle and pain, and there is nothing that is not subject to God.

Third, the statements against Tyre and Egypt speak against presumption by all nations and their leaders. There is a great temptation for leaders of all persuasions to believe that they are in control of what may happen and so are able to dispose of people and things as they see fit. The consequence is often to the detriment of people, both individuals and groups, and the environment.

Whenever leaders and nations refuse to accept any authority higher than themselves, people and the environment are at risk.For people it may lead to denial of their rights in the name of patriotism, economic and/or social poverty as resources are devoted to self-aggrandisement or military power, political oppression of people by their own leaders or by another power, limiting progress toward peace in the world through refusal to accept the legitimate claims of others or to accept responsibility for the effect of their actions on others. To claim one's own position is to provoke immediately a counter claim by another nation or consortium of nations which not only may bring about conflict at one level or another but, by the shift in power which so often occurs, makes a nonsense of the claim.

For the environment, if there is an unwillingness to accept that the things of nature are given, often are not renewable and, where they are renewable, need to be treated with care to maintain a balance between use and replenishment, harsh effects will follow. We may use our knowledge and skills to increase what nature provides for our well-being but we must be aware that this of itself may lead to gross exploitation of resources in ways that result in destruction of those resources and disregard for the generations to come.

Pharaoh not only claimed to own the Nile, but to have made it. His danger and ours is that he may then put in place his rules for the use of this resource rather than respect the rules that nature has in place. In Australia we see the result of such an attitude to the land. Large tracts of land have been destroyed by erosion which came about through people removing the native vegetation, cultivating by incorrect methods, and overcropping and overgrazing. Wind and rain, those essentials for maintaining the land in good, productive condition, then became destroyers so that there is less land suitable for production.

We would not say that we made the land but we do say in words and actions that the land is ours and we may do with it as we will. Individuals and nations have to face the consequences of this arrogant attitude.

Ezekiel reminds us that, in spite of all claims to pre-eminence, God is over all. Refusal to accept this leads to disruption and distortion of our relationship with God and with one another.

New life for Israel
33–39

A new section of the book of Ezekiel, containing mainly messages of hope for the exiles in Babylon (33.21–22), begins at chapter 33. It is significant that words of hope were placed after the threats of judgement and punishment had been fulfilled by the fall of Jerusalem and the exile of its people. Those events of judgement and punishment against the disobedient people of Israel showed that God was faithful to the covenant relationship with its promises of blessing for the obedient and cursing (punishment) for the disobedient (Deut. 28.3–68; Lev.26.3–39), and confirmed that God's promises could be relied on. God's action also showed the effectiveness of Ezekiel as a prophet. The judgement and punishment he had promised in God's name had fallen on the people. When he turned to words of promise, hope and consolation, he could be listened to with confidence

Hope for the exiles
33–37

The prophet as watchman
33.1–9

The watchman was an important person in times of war as it was his responsibility to warn the people when they were about to be attacked so that they could take refuge in the city and defend it. Ezekiel was commanded to remind the people of the role and responsibility of the watchman, and of their responsibility to act on the warning delivered by the watchman. If they failed to do so, the watchman was not to be blamed. If, however, the watchman failed to give the warning and people were killed, the watchman was responsible, and would be held to be so by God (vv.2–6).

The last part of v.6 forms a transition to the commission to the prophet to be a watchman for the Israelites (vv.7–9). As in 3.16–19, which almost duplicates this passage, the prophet's task was to pass on God's warnings to any person whom God had sentenced to death because of their wickedness, and to attempt to persuade them to change their ways. If the prophet did this, he would save his own life. If he failed to give the warning, he would be held responsible for the person's death. The task of the prophet was truly awesome. In the context of ch.3 the saying about the watchman pointed to the warnings which follow in chs.4–24 (32). In this new context the saying points back to the earlier passage to emphasise that the people were warned but they did not repent, therefore they were in exile. It is, therefore, a powerful reminder that the words of the prophet had been fulfilled, which has important implications for the words of hope in the following chapters. It suggests that the prophet who was true in warning the people of coming disaster would also be true in telling of God's intention to persevere with the people and return them to their homeland.

Individual responsibility and the freedom to repent
33.10–20

The warning of the watchman to the wicked *to give up his ways* (v.9) is taken up here with a discussion similar to that on the righteous and unrighteous man in ch.18. In this case it is introduced with the recollection of a complaint against God by the exiles that the burden of their sin brought them suffering and left no hope for life (v.10). The response was that God did not desire their death, rather, God wanted them to repent, and called them to repent (v.11).

The discussion on repentance in vv.12–16 is similar to 18.21–24, but the case of the *righteous person* who *transgresses* is treated before that of the *wicked person who mends his ways* to highlight that repentance; to *mend his ways* (v.12) and do *what is just and right* (v.16), would bring life instead of death to the wicked. This was an important message to the exiles who were in Babylon because of the evil they had done (see chs.4–24). A righteous person who committed evil would not be saved by his righteous deeds but would die because of the evil he had done (vv.12–13). However, a wicked man, on whom the sentence of death had been pronounced, would live and not die if he repented (vv.14–16). Those who claimed that this action of God was unjust (*without principle*) were assured that God would *judge each one according to his deeds*, which is the principle of justice (v.20; compare vv.17–20 with 18.25–30).

News of the fall of Jerusalem
33.21–22

These verses originally followed 24.24 to give a dramatic climax to the first stage of the prophet's message of judgement and punishment and to mark the beginning of the second stage with words of hope and renewal. They were displaced from ch.24 when the oracles against the nations were included in the collected material.

The *twelfth year* (v.21) appears to be too late as it would mean the fugitive took eighteen months to reach Babylon, which seems unlikely. There is some evidence for *eleventh year*, which allows for a journey of about six months. This would not be an unreasonable time for a fugitive to make the journey.

Receipt of the news that Jerusalem had fallen signified the renewal of the commission to the prophet to speak God's word to the people, as the release from dumbness shows (v.22). The message he had to proclaim would be from that time directed to those in exile, as in the chapters that follow.

Against those who remained in Jerusalem
33.23–29

The first prophetic statement placed after the account of Ezekiel's receipt of the news of the fall of Jerusalem is one of indictment and judgement on those who were left in the city after its fall and the deportation of some of its inhabitants. Those who were left behind claimed they were the rightful inheritors of the land (v.24). Their claim was based not only on the absence of other claimants, but also on the precedent of Abraham, who received the land as a promise from God and who was promised many descendants (Gen.12.1–3,7; 13.14–17; 15.17–21; 17.5–8; 22.15–18; Deut.9.5). They were the descendants of Abraham and they were in the land, therefore the land was theirs.

Implicit in this claim over the land was the claim that those who remained in Jerusalem were the continuing people of God. This claim was strongly rejected by Ezekiel on the grounds that they did not exhibit the behaviour of the people of God; rather, they were people who were doing things which were a denial of relationship with God (vv.25–26). The unacceptable acts of which the people were accused are also to be found in the lists used in the discussion on the righteous and unrighteous man in ch.18.

The prophet proclaimed that, rather than inherit the land, those who remained in Jerusalem would be destroyed. Destruction would come upon them in the form of *sword, wild beasts* and *pestilence* (v.27. For similar forms see 5.12; 6.11,12; 7.15; 12.16; 14.21). The land would be without people and become *a desolate waste* because of their actions (v.28–29).

This passage makes two points. First, those who were left in Jerusalem had not escaped the judgement and punishment of God; they would still be judged for their actions against God. Second, those who were in exile in Babylon, having been judged and suffered punishment, were to be seen as the continuing people of God. Judgement and punishment were the way to repentance and forgiveness.

The exiles' appreciation of the prophet
33.30–33

This is a direct address to the prophet who had been shown to be a successful prophet by the fall of Jerusalem. He was a popular figure about whom people talked and to whom people gathered to hear what he had to say, but they paid little attention to what he said to them. They paid him compliments but treated him as little more than an entertainer rather than the proclaimer of God's word to the people. Their treatment of him might have caused the prophet to despair, but God reminded him that when his words were fulfilled, the people would know that a prophet had been among them.

The prophet was thus encouraged to faithfully continue his work. When the people saw that his words were fulfilled they would know that God had spoken through him. They would understand why events had come about and so know more of God and how they should respond to God within the relationship between God and themselves. Similarly, Isaiah resolved to 'tie up the message, ... seal the instruction with my disciples' (REB, 'so that it cannot be consulted by my disciples') so that he and his children would be 'signs and portents in Israel, sent by the Lord of Hosts ... ' (Isa.8.16,18). That is, the message he had spoken would be recognised as the prophetic word of God when it was fulfilled. The prophet's justification came with the fulfilment of his words to the people, the hope that after the destruction some would return to God, and the knowledge that God's word had been spoken. (See also Isa.6.9–10,

which recognises the frustration of the prophet who spoke to people
who did not 'understand' nor 'perceive'.)

Against the shepherds of Israel
34.1–16

Rulers were often called 'shepherds' among Israel's neighbours. In
biblical literature the title is used of God (for example, Gen.48.15;
49.24; Pss.23; 80.1; Isa.40.11), and of the rulers of Israel, especially in
Jeremiah (2.8; 3.15; 10.21; 22.22 [reading 'shepherds' with Hebrew];
23.1–4; 50.6). For Jeremiah the shepherds were held responsible for
what happened to the people. In most cases he criticised them for
leading the people astray, especially in 23.1–4, which appears to be
closely linked with Ezek.34. 'Shepherd' could be an honourable title,
as is shown in Jer.3.15, which speaks of 'shepherds after my own
heart'. Ezekiel also used the term in a positive way in 34.23, where it
is said that David *will care for them* (Israel) *and be their shepherd* (see
also 37.24).

34.1–6   The rulers of Israel were identified in the command to the
prophet to proclaim a *woe* oracle against them (v.2) because they
were like shepherds who had not fulfilled their responsibilities
toward their flock. The main point of the indictment against them
was that the shepherds cared *only for themselves* and not for the flock,
so that, instead of helping the weak, the sick and the crippled, and
seeking the lost, they had plundered the flock (vv.2–4). They had
abused their right to use the produce from the flock in return for care
of the flock. The welfare of the flock was ignored.

This neglect resulted in the scattering of the flock which, without a
shepherd, became prey to wild beasts and were left to wander without leadership or protection (vv.5–6). The leaders of the nation were
thus blamed for the dispersion of the people and their destruction at
the hands of the nations. They were also considered responsible for
the people's apostasy in alien cult practices, as *over all the mountains
and on every high hill* shows (see 6.13).

34.9–10   is the judgement that is to be expected after a 'woe oracle'.
Verse 9 announces judgement in terms of God's opposition to the
shepherds, a calling to account and, finally, dismissal from the task
of caring for the flock (v.10). They would be rejected by God. The
judgement statement is concluded with a promise to rescue the

sheep from the mouths of the shepherds; this gave hope to the people, but confirmed the condemnation of the rulers, who acted like ravening wolves rather than shepherds of the flock.

34.7–8   appears to be an addition made up of a repeat of v.9 and a restatement of v.5. The purpose of the addition was to emphasise the charge against the rulers (shepherds) and thus sharpen the words of the judgement which God promised.

34.11–16   The final part of this section is also presented as God's message to the people, but here it is a message of hope to an exiled and scattered people. It is also presented as a contrast between the shepherds who allowed the flock to be destroyed, and God who would act as a true shepherd to gather it and restore it. Indeed, God's actions would be the reverse of those of the rulers (shepherds) of Israel. Where the shepherds left the flock with *no one to enquire after them or search for them* (v.6), God (with the 'I' strongly emphasised to give *I myself* [REB]) promised to *take thought* (the same Hebrew word as for 'enquire', v.6) *for my sheep and search for them*. The shepherds allowed the sheep to scatter and become the prey of wild beasts (v.5) but God would search them out and rescue them (v.12), return them to their own good land (v.13), and provide them with good pasture and a place of rest (vv.14–15). Verse 14 is reminiscent of Ps.23.2 and appears to have been drawn from that psalm to emphasise the 'rest' that God would give to the restored people.

The contrast so clearly drawn in vv.11–15 pointed the exiled people to the hope they had in God, who not only had judged them so that they went into exile in Babylon and were scattered among the nations, but who also would act to restore them to their homeland and provide for them. The actions of the pre-exilic rulers (shepherds) had led to judgement and destruction, but the action of God, the true shepherd, would lead to new life.

Verse 16 completes the contrast by showing that the neglect by the shepherds, referred to in v.4, would be reversed by God, the good shepherd, and the people would be sought, restored, and cared for. This is an addition to the hope oracle in vv.11–15. It serves to summarise the characteristics of the good shepherd and to provide a transition to the next section. The transition is more clearly seen in the Hebrew text which may be translated, 'the strong I will exterminate, and I will shepherd them (my sheep) with justice'. (REB has followed the Greek.)

Judging the flock
34.17–22

The role of the shepherd in vv.17–22 is that of one who would administer justice to the flock. God would judge the sheep in accordance with their actions, specifically the strong among the flock (*rams* and *he-goats*), who not only had consumed the best pasture and water, but also spoiled what they did not want so that it was unpalatable for the weak (vv.17–19)

A similar judgement and charge is in vv.20–21. In this case it is against the *fat sheep* who used their strength to *push aside* the *weak sheep* and *scattered them*. God's action in saving the flock would also include bringing justice among its members (v.22).

These two sayings have been brought together to emphasise that the leaders of the community, as well as the rulers, would be judged for their actions against the people. They thus take up the point of indictment and judgement made in vv.3–10, but, by being placed after vv.11–16, which speak of God's saving action, they proclaim God's justice which would be known among the gathered people. Justice would be part of God's provision for the restored people.

Caring for the flock
34.23–31

God's care for the people is returned to in vv.23–31 with an important statement of relationship, *I, the Lord, shall be their God* (v.24), and significant titles used for the leader of the restored people; that is, *servant, shepherd* and *prince* (vv.23,24). These titles recall important features of traditions from Israel's past. They have been brought together so that the people would understand the type of leader God would provide for them. *My servant David* would be the *shepherd to take care of them* and be the *prince among them*.

Significant aspects of Ezekiel's understanding of the relationship between God and the restored people are shown here. First is the nature of the relationship. It will be one in which God makes a pledge to be the God of the people. This has within it an element of promise and will be, therefore, a source of hope for the people. God has chosen them and *shall be their God*, recalling the covenant relationship which was characteristic of pre-exilic Israel and is taken up also in Ezek.16.59–63; 37.26. (Compare with Ezek.36.24–28 and Jer.31.31–41.)

Second, the designation of *David my servant* as the *one shepherd to take care of them* (v.23; for the term *shepherd* see the introduction to the discussion of 34.1–16) recalls 'Servant of the Lord', a title of honour conferred on those who gave special service to God; for example, Abraham ('my servant' Gen.26.24), Moses (Exod.14.31; Deut.34.5; Josh.1.15; 8.31,33 and several other places in Joshua), Joshua (Josh.24.29) and David ('my servant', II Sam.3.18; 7.5,8; I Kings 11.13,32–38). All of these people were notable for their close relationship with God and their roles in leading God's people. The use of *my servant David* here indicates that the restored people would have a leader of David's line and of David's loyalty and obedience to God. This characteristic would ensure that the *shepherd* who would lead God's restored people would be a shepherd of care, justice and right relationship between God and people and among the people.

Third, the promise that David would be their *shepherd* and *prince among them* recalls the tradition of David, the shepherd whom God took 'to be a prince over my people Israel' (see II Sam.7.8; a different Hebrew word is used for *prince* in this passage [it may also be translated 'ruler'], but it appears that the author of Ezek.34.24 was intending to draw on the connection with David the shepherd who became a 'ruler' and combined these two functions in the one person), and the promise that David would start a dynasty to rule Israel. It is significant that the word *prince*, rather than 'king', is used here, for it indicates a break from the kings of the pre-exilic period, whom Ezekiel charged with responsibility for Israel's disobedience, judgement, and destruction (see e.g. 34.1–6). There is no suggestion that the historical David would be brought back to life; rather, one of David's line, an inheritor of the promise to David and the traditions of David the faithful ruler, was promised.

Fourth, there would be *one shepherd*, signifying that there would be one kingdom, not the two divided kingdoms which existed for much of the period of the monarchy. The restoration would be of Israel, the people of God.

34.25–30 The figure of the shepherd and the flock or sheep has been abandoned in this added section, which has direct concern with the situation of the returned exiles. Verses 25–27 describe the conditions in which the restored people would live with the Lord as *their God* and David as their prince and shepherd. The list of things the people would enjoy has been drawn from the promises made to those who were faithful to the covenant relationship with God in Lev.26.3–13.

In the (new) covenant, God would ensure *peace and prosperity* for
the people by keeping them safe from *wild beasts* (v.25) and from
enemies (v.27), and by providing for their needs (vv.26,27). This
theme has been restated in vv.28–29, which has also drawn on
Lev.26.3–13.

The section concludes by taking up the promise that God would
make a covenant with them (the people, v.25) in a form which includes
both the divine and human sides of the relationship (v.30). This
would be the source of the people's hope while in exile, and the basis
of their life as the restored people of God when they returned to their
homeland.

34.31   concludes the whole chapter. It returns to the figure of the
shepherd and the flock, and includes elements of the covenant
formula, *my flock … your God*. The chapter is clearly composite in
nature, but the last verse has brought its different parts together in
such a way that it addressed the needs of the exiles. It gave an
explanation of why they were in exile, an assurance that God was
with them in exile, and a pledge that the scattered people would be
gathered and returned to the land of God's promise.

Against Edom
  35.1–15

This chapter, with its words against Edom, appears to be out of place
in a section which proclaims restoration for the exiles. It has been
placed here to give a contrast with the oracle about the mountains of
Israel in ch.36 (*the hill-country of Seir* will be destroyed, salvation will
come to *the mountains of Israel*), and to accentuate that action against
foreign nations would be a prelude to the restoration of Israel. Edom
was an obvious target for such an oracle, as it had played a part in
the downfall of Judah, and had occupied part of Judah's territory
after the fall of Jerusalem (see on 25.12–14 above). This point is made
in 36.5 '… *against the rest of the nations, and against Edom above all*.

The statement is in four parts following an introduction in which
the prophet was commanded to *face towards the hill-country of Seir and
prophesy against it* (v.2). Such an action by a prophet, of itself, conveyed God's action against that territory. The *hill-country of Seir* was
a mountain range in the territory of Edom, which is equated to Edom
(*the whole of Edom*) in v.15.

35.3–9 The first part (vv.3–4) states the action God would take against the *hill-country of Seir*. It would be destroyed totally. Reasons for this action are not given, but the way in which the first and second parts have been put together makes the reason given for God's action in the second part (v.5) apply to both parts. That is, the maintenance of an ancient feud, a reference to the Esau and Jacob tradition (Gen.24.19–34), and the use of it as an excuse to take revenge on Israel when the destruction of Jerusalem presented the opportunity, was the cause of God's action against Edom. The reason is presented in the form of a charge, beginning with *for* (or 'because'), which is followed by the consequential action of judgement, introduced by *therefore* and the oath *as I live, says the Lord God*. As in the first part, the action of God would be the devastation of the hill-country of Seir (vv.6–9).

35.10–15 The charge in the third part is that the hill-country of Seir had laid claim to the territory of both Israel and Judah (vv.10 and 12). In the judgement which follows God promised, again by oath, to do to the hill-country of Seir as it had done to the two kingdoms (vv.10–12). A similar threat is made in v.15 in the words of judgement in the fourth part of the statement (vv.13–15). In this latter case the charge is that the hill-country of Seir had boasted against God (v.13) for which it would be judged and made desolate (v.14,15b). The text of v. 14 is difficult. An explanation has been added in v.15a (absent from the Greek text) to help the reader understand what was meant. The passage concludes with the identification of *the hill-country of Seir* with the land of Edom, and the reinforcing declaration that *the whole of Edom* would be made desolate (v.15).

The charges against Edom are similar to those made in other oracles against the nations; that is, Edom, taking revenge against Israel (vv.5, compare 25.12); Tyre, taking possession of the land of Israel (v.10, compare 26.2); Tyre and Egypt, boasting and arrogance (v.13, compare chs.28 and 31).

Each part of the passage concludes with the identification formula *you will know that I am the Lord* (vv.4,9,12,15 [all], and the variation in v.11b). The action of God was to be not only judgement on Edom, but also a demonstration through which God would be known.

To the mountains of Israel
36.1–15

The first part of ch.36 is connected to ch.35, as noted above. This connection has been achieved by the specific association in v.5 of Edom with the nations which acted against Israel. It is probable that this reference to Edom is an addition to make the connection explicit. The Hebrew of *the whole of Edom* (35.15) and *Edom above all* (36.5) is the same except for one letter which probably represents a scribal error. There is also a play on the words *hill-country of Seir* (lit. Mount Seir, 35.1,7,15) and *mountains of Israel* (36.1,4,8) which indicates that the two are to be taken together.

There is a connection with ch.6 in which the mountains of Israel were condemned because of the disobedience of the people, but here, in the context of the promised punishment being experienced in exile, the message has been reversed to convey hope. The mountains would be resettled with the people of Israel, for God, who promised judgement and punishment in the pre-exilic period, now promised restoration in the new circumstances of exile.

This passage was formed from separate sayings to make up a statement against the nations which had oppressed Israel (vv.1–7), and a statement in which the roles of Israel and the nations were reversed and Israel's renewal proclaimed (vv.8–15).

36.1–7 The primary statement is in v.2, the 'boasting' cry of the victors over the vanquished, spoken by Israel's enemies. This has been elaborated in vv.3–4 to describe the way the nations gloated over conquered Israel and so emphasise that, for the sake of divine honour (*my jealousy*), God had to speak out against the nations (v.5). After a further preparatory statement (v.6), the judgement of God is given in the declaration that the nations would endure taunting (v.7). They would have the experience which had been Israel's.

Similar charges against Israel's enemies who profited from its fall are found in chs.25 (vv.3,6, concerning the Ammonites), and 26 (v.2, concerning Tyre). Charges of 'arrogance' and 'god-like airs' brought against Tyre are found in 28.2,6. In ch.36 the charge was a further sign of hope for exiled Israel. The positions of Israel and the nations would be reversed.

36.8–11 This reversal of positions is proclaimed in terms of the homecoming of the people. It was near, as had been the day of judgement in the pre-exilic proclamation (7.7). In contrast to the description in vv.3–4, and to God's action against the *hill-country of Seir* (35.2–4), the *mountains of Israel* would be restored, fruitful, and prosperous again. Hope was re-affirmed.

36.12–15   The final part of this passage is a series of additions to vv.8–11. Verse 12 summarises the content of vv.8–11 and makes the transition from the *mountains* (vv.8–11) to the *land* (vv.13–14). The last words of v.12 have been taken up in vv.13–14 to proclaim God's action to reverse Israel's reputation as a land which devoured its own people. It would not happen again. That was God's assurance. A further summary statement of encouragement, assuring the people of God's continued care and protection has been added in v.15.

Renewal of the people of Israel
36.16–32

These verses present a strong statement of hope for exiled Israel and an explicit reference to the basis of that hope in the action of God. The first part summarises what had happened to the Israelites to the point of their experience of the exile (vv.16–21). They had their own land but they defiled it by the uncleanness of their life (v.17). The words used for this refer to the cultic impurity of a woman at the time of menstruation and draw on legislation in the Holiness Code which aims at preventing defilement of the sanctuary (Lev.15.19–30). This thought has been extended in v.18 to make explicit that the people had defiled the land with their violence and idolatry; *blood they poured out on the land, idols with which they defiled it.* The land was therefore ritually unclean. To cleanse it, God removed the people from it and dispersed them among the nations (compare Lev.26.40–43). This was God's justice in action against the people (v.19c).

36.20–21   God's action in scattering the people among the nations caused God's holy name to be profaned and treated as a common thing by the nations. This happened because the nations looked at Israel, exiled from the land God had promised it, and reflected on the ability of God to maintain the people in the land. God was concerned that this reflected on his *holy name* (see also on 20.8–9, above) and raised the question for the exiles, 'How could God forgive a people who had been driven from the land they had defiled?'

36.22–23   answers the question. God would act, not because of the people, but for *the sake of* God's *name* so that it was clear to all that the new beginning for Israel would be both by God and from God, in accordance with the nature and character of God (see Num.14.11–23). In that action God's holiness would be shown and the nations would *know that I am the Lord, says the Lord God.*

36.24–32   God's action to save Israel is elaborated by the description of how God would cleanse and change the people and the land. First, the people would be returned from the nations to their own land (v.24), then they would go through three cleansing rituals to renew them and enable them to be obedient to God. Sprinkling with *pure water* (v.25) suggests ritual cleansing and recalls Ps.51.7, which refers to sprinkling and cleansing of the worshipper. A new heart and spirit would be given. As in 11.19–20, this promised the renewal of the very being of the people so that they would be able to respond to God and be obedient (v.26). Finally the spirit they were to be given was God's spirit which would enable the people to obey God in fulfilment of the covenant requirements. That is, God would take a new initiative by providing the motive force for the people to respond to God's action with the obedience God required. With the ritual cleansing and renewing complete, the people would live in the land God had given. The seal for this is the covenant formula *you will be my people, and I shall be your God* (vv.27–28).

The cleansed (*saved*) Israel would have a fruitful land in which God would *command grain* to grow and *make fruit trees to bear*. There would be no more famine (vv.28–29). This fruitfulness of the land would remind Israel of earlier days and cause self-loathing for what it had done (v.31). The conclusion (v.32) brings the two parts of vv.16–31 together by reminding the people that what they would enjoy would come, not from any action on their part, but by God's action on their behalf. The realisation of this would produce a feeling of *shame and disgrace* among the people.

36.33–38   Two further developments of the saying, *When they see that I reveal my holiness through you*, (v.23) have been added to vv.16–32. The first (vv.33–36) is in terms of the resettlement of the land and the rebuilding of its cities and is a development of the promise of v.10 to emphasise God's action in reversing the fortunes of exiled Israel. The mention of the *garden of Eden* suggests that this action was to be seen as a new creation, conveying the renewing action of God in restoring exiled Israel to its homeland (see Isa.40.12–31). Again the nations would recognise this as the action of God.

The second development (vv.37–38) also points to the renewed Israel. God's willingness to allow the *Israelites to pray to me for help* (v.37), a sign of the acceptance of the people, reversed the refusal to be 'consulted' by the 'elders of Israel' (14.3; 20.3), which was part of God's rejection of the disobedient people. (Note, 'consult' and 'pray' translate the same Hebrew word in these references.) *Ruined cities* of Israel filled with people as Jerusalem was filled with sheep for sacrifice on a festival day also speaks of restoration (v.38). The large numbers of animals said to have been sacrificed by Solomon at the dedication of the temple may have been the inspiration for this comment (I Kings 8.63).

The valley of dry bones
37.1–14

This passage, the best known in the book of Ezekiel, describes a vision the prophet had which spectacularly portrayed the renewing power of God. It is not surprising that it has been the subject of many artistic presentations and interpretations.

The first part of the account (vv.1–10) describes a vision of dry, human bones, scattered over a plain, which were assembled and given life as the prophet spoke God's word over them. The second part (vv.11–14) interprets the vision to the despairing exiles.

The vision takes up and deals with the despair expressed in the quoted words of the people in v.11, *Our bones are dry, our hope is gone, and we are cut off*. Presentation of the vision suggests a battlefield where the bodies of the slain had been left without proper burial so that a great number of bones remained to be scattered and become *very dry*. It is not possible, nor is it necessary, to identify such a battlefield. The vision was a response to the words of the people. However, it does appear that Ezekiel drew on the words of Jeremiah who spoke of judgement against the officials and inhabitants of Jerusalem who would be dishonoured by the scattering of their bones like 'dung spread over the ground' (Jer.8.1–3).

117

The presentation of the vision emphasises three things:

First, the despair of the people (the bones were *very dry*, v.2).

Second, the dependence of the people on the power of God to effect a change for them, shown in the answer to the question, *can these bones live? Only you, Lord God, know that* (v.3).

Third, the power of the prophet's word spoken at God's direction. The dry bones were to *hear the word of the Lord* (v.4), which, as it was spoken by the prophet, brought the reassembly of the bones and their reconstitution as bodies with flesh and skin (vv.7–8).

The account is structured to make maximum use of the dramatic character of the vision and so catch up the deep feelings of the people, to change them from people of profound despair to people with confidence and a sustaining hope. Its death to life message was particularly appropriate for the people in exile who considered themselves as good as dead.

Occurrence of the Hebrew word *ruah* in this passage is important. It is used for *spirit of the Lord* (REB, *his spirit*) in v.1 (also in 11.5) as the means by which God conveyed the prophet to the place of the vision. In vv.5,8 and 10 it is translated *breath*, the breath that brings life. God had the prophet say to the bones, *I am going to put the breath of life in you, and you will live* (v.5). Part way through his prophesying over the bones, Ezekiel saw that the bodies were complete, but *there was no breath in them* (v.8). Finally, after the prophet prophesied to the wind (*ruah*) , it came as four winds from each quarter to *breathe into these slain* (v.9), and *breath entered them, and they came to life* (v.10). The *wind* is to be seen as signifying God's action in imparting the life-giving breath to the lifeless bodies. The use of *ruah* brought together the action of God in the work of the prophet (v.1), through agency of the wind (v.9), and in bringing life to the bodies (v.10). The understanding that only God could breathe life into a lifeless body has behind it the action of God in breathing the 'breath of life' into the lifeless body of the human being God had created from the 'dust of the ground' (Gen.2.7).

37.11–14   The interpretation of the vision is in two parts, vv.11 and 14, and vv.12–13. The first applied the vision account to the exiles who despaired of their situation. They were dry bones, without hope, and life was ended (v.11). But, the prophet said, God who could give life to dry bones could put *my spirit* in them so that they would have life and return to their land (v.14). It is a statement of hope in God where there is apparently none. God who had spoken would also act (v.14).

The second interpretation changed the base thought of the vision from dry bones scattered in a field to bodies in their graves. It is a later interpretation which proclaimed God's power to give life to exiled Israel, even if it was as bodies sealed in their graves (vv.12–13).

Ruah occurs again as a catchword in v.14 (*my spirit*, also in 36.27; 39.29) to take up God's action in giving the exiles life, settling them in their homeland, and thus causing them to know that God's spoken word was fulfilled. This forms the fitting conclusion to the vision and its interpretations which proclaim the renewing power of the spirit of God among the exiled people. They would be renewed.

Israel reunited
37.15–28

The prophet was commanded to perform a symbolic action to signify the reunification of the two former kingdoms of Israel (vv.16–17). Two interpretations of this action have been given in vv.18–19 and 20–28.

The symbolic action involved the prophet taking two pieces of wood, writing on one Judah and on the other Joseph and bringing them together in his hand so that they appeared to be one piece of wood. Although REB interprets the Hebrew word for 'wood' as a *leaf of a wooden tablet*, it is more likely that a stick or stave is meant; that is, pieces of wood the prophet could hold so that they were joined together in his hand. Explanatory comments have been added at a later time to clarify who was intended by the names *Judah* and *Joseph*. The names were meant to be inclusive, as is shown by *and the Israelites associated with him* after *Judah* and *the leaf of Ephraim and all the Israelite tribes* after *Joseph*.

37.18–19 The first explanation, with the addition of words similar to those in v.17, says that God would join the two former kingdoms and make them one.

37.20–23 A second explanation is connected to the symbolic action by reference to the pieces of wood (v.20) and has retained the thought of the one nation. There will be one kingdom and one king (v.22). This has been extended with a statement of God's intention to return the exiles to their homeland and to restore them (vv.21,23), which is similar to 36.24–28, and marks another strong statement of the action God would take to renew the relationship between God and the returned people. All those things that denied the relationship would be removed, and it could be restated in terms of the covenant formula *they will be my people, I shall be their God* (v.23).

37.24–28   The second explanation has been subject to further interpretation. The word *king*, which occurs appropriately in connection with *kingdoms* in v.22, has been re-interpreted in terms of 34.23–24 by identifying the king with David, the shepherd-prince (vv.24–25; see the comments above on 34.23–24). The permanence of the restoration and the place of the people in their relationship with God is emphasised by recalling the promise of the land to Jacob and his descendants (Gen.35.12), the ongoing line of princes of David's line, and the *everlasting covenant* (vv.25–26). With each of these recollections the prophet emphasised that what the people would be given would be for all time; they would live *for ever* in the land given to Jacob and where their forebears had lived, David would be *their prince forever*, and the covenant would be *everlasting* (vv.25–26), all of which recalls the unconditional covenants God made with Noah (Gen.9.16) and Abraham (Gen.17.7). The *sanctuary in their midst for all time* was a further important promise of God's continuing presence with the people and a symbol of the ongoing covenant relationship of v.27. The sanctuary also would be a sign to the nations that Israel was being maintained as a people sacred to God (v.28).

Against Gog of Magog
38.1–39.29

Ezekiel's use of the material of his predecessors has been seen earlier in the book (e.g. chs.16 and 23). Here he has used the theme of the threat of an enemy nation coming against Israel which is found in Isaiah (5.26–30) and Jeremiah (4–6). He has, however, changed it from a proclamation of an enemy threat as God's way of punishing disobedient Israel, to an affirmation of protection for the restored, renewed and obedient Israel through God's intention to destroy the nation which would seek to crush Israel.

The text consists of three basic statements concerning Gog and the defeat of his armies (38.1–9; 39.1–5, 17–20), to which have been added blocks of material intended to broaden the application of the chapters to a later time.

The position of the chapters in the book is puzzling. We might have expected to find them with the oracles against the nations (chs.25–32) because of some similarity in theme. Their position between chs.37 and 40 interrupts what may be seen as a logical continuity from the statement on the importance of the sanctuary for the returned and restored exiles (37.26–28) and the reconstruction of the temple (chs.40–48). It may be that they owe their position to the need to offer assurance that the people whom God had brought out of exile, restored to their homeland, renewed, and given the sanctuary as a sign of God's continued presence, could rely on God for protection in time of threat. Certainly the later additions aim to show God triumphant against enemies who would threaten God's people.

One effect of chs.38–39 is to form a dramatic interlude between the promise of a covenant of peace (37.26) and the vision of the new temple (40–48) and so to heighten the impact of the temple vision.

There have been many suggestions about whom Gog represents historically, but a positive identification is not possible. The major point for the prophet was to present a picture of a leader who had great forces at his disposal which he would use in an attack on Israel. Gog was from Magog (v.2), a nation referred to in the table of nations as one of the sons of Japheth (Gen.10.2). He is called the *chief prince* (rather than *prince of Rosh* as in REB) of *Tubal and Meshech*, and the sons of Japheth, nations to the north of Israel (vv.2,3). In addition he led the forces of Gomer and Beth-togarmah, neighbours of Tubal and Meshech (v.6).

The prophet was called to turn *towards Gog*, a way of expressing God's opposition to a person or place (compare 6.2; 25.2; 28.21; 29.2) and tell him that God would direct him, with all his forces, to invade the gathered and restored Israel. At the appropriate time he would advance like an irresistible *hurricane* (vv.3–9). Verse 5 is a later addition which includes nations to the east and south of Israel (Persia, Cush and Put) in the force to come against Israel. The addition increased the size of the attacking force and so made God's victory over these forces of world importance.

38.10–23 Three additions which develop the base text follow. Verses 10–13 elaborate on God's action in calling Gog to invade

Israel. Gog is pictured planning to take advantage of a people recently resettled in their homeland after a period of exile. They would be without defences, *open villages ... undefended by walls or barred gates* (v.11), but they would be wealthy (vv.12,13) and so ripe for plunder; a very attractive prospect to an ambitious enemy power, especially as it would lead to trade with such noted traders as Sheba, Dedan and Tarshish (v.13). There is also a suggestion that the land would be worth taking for itself. It would give honour to its conqueror and possessor for it was *the very centre of the world* (v.12). This belief that Jerusalem was of such importance as to be thought of as the centre of the world is also found in 5.5. It is a comment on the Israelite belief that their land was favoured by God above all others.

A summary of vv.2–9 is given in vv.14–16. Its purpose is to make plain that Gog's advance against Israel would be at God's instigation; that through it the nations would know God in the destruction of Gog, for this would demonstrate God's holiness (v.16b).

The last addition begins with a further, later addition (v.17). It looks back from later time to *the prophets, who prophesied in those days unceasingly* that God would bring a powerful enemy against Israel, and says their words would be fulfilled in Gog. This may be a reference to unfulfilled prophecies or a reapplication of prophetic statements which threatened invasion and devastation (for example, Jer.4.5–6.26 where the invading power is not named).

The invasion by Gog and his massive forces would be dealt with by God (vv.18–23). As in vv.10 (*at that time*, REB), 14 and 19, the phrase *on that day* (v.18) suggests the 'day of the Lord', the day of God's reckoning for unfaithful Israel and/or foreign nations which opposed God (see above on 7.5–9). In this instance it would be a day of reckoning for Gog against whom God's *wrath will boil over* (v.18). In it there would be a world-shattering display of power in earthquake, *pestilence, bloodshed,* flood and *hailstones, fire and brimstone* (vv.19–22). Fear would strike all creatures so that Gog's men would turn on one another with their swords. So Gog and his armies would be destroyed and in the action of destroying Gog, God would be shown to be *great and holy,* and *known* among the nations (v.23).

39.1–5 The second basic statement continues the stress on God's initiative in dealing with Gog seen in 38.1–9. God is the one who would lead Gog from his distant homeland to the mountains of Israel where he, his allies and their armies would be totally destroyed and their bodies left as *food for birds of prey and wild beasts* (vv.2–5). It is notable that Israel would have no part in this action. God's responsibility for the destruction of this great enemy is stressed by the repetition of 'I' in God's address to Gog; *I am against you, I shall turn you round, I shall lead you, I shall strike the bow from your left hand, I shall give you as food, it is I who have spoken*; and it would certainly happen, for what was spoken was *the word of the Lord God* (v.5).

39.6–16   As with the first part of the basic statement, this second part has been developed with a number of additions, vv.6–16. Verses 6–8 give again the reason for God's activity against Gog and his forces; that God's name would be known among the nations and no longer be profaned among God's people Israel. This latter statement reverses the charge that Israel profaned God's name among the nations by its disobedience (36.20–23). The renewed and restored Israel would honour the name of God.

The significance for Israel of God's victory is shown in the next two additions. First, the Israelites would take the weapons of the fallen and destroy them by using them for fuel (vv.9–10). This is in line with the tradition that God would burn weapons of war and soldiers' clothing as represented in Isa.9.5 and Ps.46.9. So large would be the enemy force that their weapons would provide the people with fuel *for seven years*, an undoubted a sign of the magnitude of God's victory and the retribution which may be visited on those who plundered Israel. The use of *seven*, the number which symbolises completeness, suggests peace for Israel, for the means of war would be completely destroyed.

Second, provision was to be made for burial of the huge number of dead bodies (vv.11–16). This is in contradiction to the base text in v.4 and vv.17–20 which provides for the corpses to be eaten by birds and wild beasts. The provision for burial is in two parts. Verses 11–13 deal with the burial which, with purification of the land, would take *seven months*. Although the people would not take part in the defeat and destruction of Gog and his forces, their involvement in the burial operations would be memorable as the day when honour would be won for God.

The place of burial is not clear. The REB translation *instead of a burial ground in Israel* is doubtful (v.11); 'I will give to Gog a place for burial in Israel' is preferable. *Abarim,* the name of a range of mountains to the *east of the Dead Sea,* is arrived at by following an amendment to the vowels of the word. As it is written in the Hebrew text it would be 'Oberim' and translated 'the valley of travellers'. Also, the sea is unidentified in the text, *Dead Sea* being arrived at by association with the mountain range of 'Abarim'. It is likely that the burial site would be in Israel. As such it would be impure and travellers would, therefore, be unable to pass through it. The importance of the place would be noted by the name, *Valley of Gog's Horde*. This may be a play on the name 'valley of the son of Hinom', a place of infamy associated with pagan worship rites and desecrated by King Josiah by making it a place for burning refuse and disposal of corpses (II Kings 23.8). The Hebrew of the two names is similar and suggests a play on word sounds.

The second part of the provision for burial (vv.14–16) deals with the need to *purify the land* which had been contaminated by the mass of dead bodies and envisages a group appointed to identify human remains and ensure they were suitably buried so that the land would be purified. This addition has been made to satisfy the priestly need for purification and may be later than other additions in chs.38–39.

39.17–20   The final section of the basic statement is the conclusion to God's action in calling Gog and his forces to destruction. It is the account of their dishonourable end, which would not be in burial, but in having the remains of the great mass of Gog's forces left on the open ground to be eaten by birds and wild animals invited by God for the purpose. This would be the ultimate indignity for Gog and his great armies whose bodies would serve as a sacrificial meal, prepared by God for the birds and animals. The indignity is compounded in that it represents a reversal of the usual practice when animals were sacrificed and eaten. In this case the birds and animals would eat human flesh which would take the place of *rams, sheep, he-goats, bulls, and buffaloes.*

39.21–29   gives a conclusion to chs. 38–39 and a summary of Israel's exile and restoration at God's hand. God's action against Gog would bring glory to God and cause the Israelites to acknowledge God (vv.21,22). Verses 23–24 explain the exile in terms of Israel's unfaithfulness and the deserved punishment with which God afflicted the people. But that was not the end of God's dealing with Israel (Jacob), it would be restored because of God's *compassion* and because God is *jealous for* his *name* (v.25; see 36.16–23). Although the REB translation follows other translations and scholars in rendering v.26 'they will forget their shame' the emendation to give this translation should not be followed. Rather, we should read 'they will remember (bear) *their shame and all their unfaithfulness to me'*. That is, their past would be the warning they needed to carry with them into their future relationship with God. God would restore and provide for the people, but God would also require of them the response of faithfulness. Remembering their past and its consequences would help them to be faithful and to be grateful for God's mercy toward them.

This conclusion forms a bridge to the next major part of the book, the vision of the new temple and provision for the cultic life of the restored people.

HOPE AND RESTORATION

The overall statement of chs.33–39 is one of hope; hope in the God who said to Israel in Egypt, 'I am the Lord your God' and who then delivered Israel out of the land of slavery to the promised land of 'milk and honey' (20.5,6).

The structure of the section shows the need for hope, the people were in despair. It shows the source of hope is God, who would act for the people. It shows also that the substance of hope is forgiveness, restoration to their own land and renewal of their life and relationship with God. The message of hope in Ezekiel comes as a direct response to expressions of failure and despair when the people faced the end which the destruction of Jerusalem and exile to Babylon represented. The people's complaint, *We are burdened by our sins and offences; we are pining away because of them, and despair of life* (33.10), leads in to statements of hope in the verses and chapters that follow. (The same process may be seen in 11.13, followed by 11.14–21, and 20.32, followed by 20.33–44.)

In these chapters reference is made to different aspects of Israel's life which had been dealt with in earlier parts of the book – warning, judgement on Jerusalem and the leaders of the people, punishment and hope in repentance – each one reminding the people of God's actions within their relationship with God. This establishes continuity in the relationship as a basis for hope. God was still dealing with them. The one who had judged and punished them still cared for them and would act for them. In proclaiming this Ezekiel pointed the people to hope in God.

This hope is spelled out as the prophet moves on from a call to repentance in 33.12–20 to proclaim that God would act directly on behalf of the people. The major emphasis is on what God would do:

1. remove the false shepherds (rulers) who had exploited the sheep (people);

2. appoint, from the line of the ideal king David, a prince to care for the people;

3. make a covenant to ensure peace and prosperity;

4. gather the people, purify them with water and give them a new heart and a new spirit so they could respond to God;

5. put flesh on a mass of dry bones and breath into their bodies to raise them to life;

6. restore the people to their own land and establish them with an everlasting covenant;

7. defeat and destroy the great enemy Gog of Magog.

The people could rely on God. Hope was in God who would do everything to restore Israel.

This strong emphasis on the action of God does not do away with the need for repentance. It is an important part of restoration of the relationship with God, but it may not take place at the beginning of that process. That is, as 36.24–32 shows, repentance in the form of recalling *your wicked conduct and evil deeds, loathing yourselves because of your wrongdoing and your abominations* and *feeling the shame and disgrace of your ways* (vv.31–32) may be the response by the people who had been brought back, cleansed and renewed by God (vv.25–28). The initiative of God is preserved and the need for the people to turn to God (repent) is acknowledged.

The two elements in this hope proclaimed by Ezekiel have timeless importance for humankind. First there is the call to repent and the assurance that those who turn to God will be forgiven. He powerfully makes the point that God's offer of relationship does not end with judgement, nor any other calamity that may befall us, but God continues to be with people to seek restoration of relationship. God is always there to welcome the one who returns, as the parable of the Lost Son so powerfully reminds us (Luke 15.11–31). This is an important part of our understanding of God and a source of confidence for those who are estranged from God to turn to God.

The second element, that forgiveness, restoration and renewal come by the action of God and the initiative of God, is a fundamental point in Ezekiel's thinking concerning the God-human relationship. Throughout chs.33–39 he emphasises the action of God on behalf of Israel. In answer to despair God says, 'See what I have done, what I am doing and what I will do for you; in this is your hope.' No situation is so bad that hope is futile, not dispossession, exile, slavery, nor even death, for God is seen to be active in all these to bring new life.

So, what God does in renewal of the relationship is constant. God is with the people whatever the situation or the place, and God is acting for the people. The people may repent; that is, turn to God when judgement threatens, or when judgement is pronounced and punishment is being suffered, or when it is realised that renewal has come by the action of God. Whenever it happens, some form of repentance is part of the renewing of the relationship and always it is in response to God's action, for the initiative is with God. This is the insight we receive from Ezekiel.

Jesus Christ is the supreme evidence of God's action for people. He is God among the people of the world, not denying what Ezekiel says, but fulfilling it, taking it to that further point of God's involvement in human affairs as one of us. His coming, his living, his dying and his resurrection are all done that we may know that we are loved and forgiven. He is, in human form, God's words of action from Ezekiel; 'I shall go, I shall gather, I shall lead, I shall feed, I shall give, I shall put, I shall make, I am going to put breath into you and you shall live.' In Christ that has been done. When we realise it has been done for us we turn to God (repent) and accept the way of love God has for us.

This is the experience of many people. They are drawn to Jesus Christ by the attractiveness of his being, or by the example of his selfless life, or by his evident self-sacrifice on the cross, or by the lives his followers live, and they are aware of being drawn into relationship with God. In the experience of that relationship they become conscious of God's action for them and of their need to respond to God in repentance and faith.

Others express the renewal of relationship with God in terms of an awareness of their lack of worth and despair at the direction their life has taken. Their response is to acknowledge God as the one to whom they are responsible, and in that to be moved to repent as the first step in forming the relationship with God who was and is always there, and then to live in faith in Jesus Christ, with the blessings he brings to his people.

Ezekiel helps us to see that God's action toward us is primary in our relationship with God. Our response relies on and follows that initiative and may be given at any point, whatever our status in the relationship at the time. In the next section Ezekiel points to the need to be active in maintaining our response to God that the relationship may be sustained.

The vision of a new temple
40–48

The final major part of the book of Ezekiel is in the form of a vision in which God gave the prophet the plan for a new temple, regulations for its ordering and provision and a new allocation of the land among the tribes of Israel. These three elements provided a structure for the life of the returned and restored people and gave a consistent emphasis on the centrality of the temple and its cult in their life.

The vision of the new temple, 40.1–43.12, is a counterpart to the vision in chs.8–11. In the earlier vision the prophet was shown the abominations of the people, especially as these related to the temple, which culminated in the glory of God leaving the temple, the sign of God's rejection of the people. In this later vision the prophet was shown the plan and dimensions of the new temple and witnessed the glory of God return to it, the sign that God would be with the restored people when they returned from exile.

43.13–48.35 emphasise the central place of the temple in the life of Israel and its importance as the means of maintaining Israel's relationship with God. As such these chapters have a close connection with chs.34–37 and the hope for a repentant people to return to their homeland and live in covenant relationship with their God.

The new temple
40.1–43.12

Introduction to the vision
40.1–4

The date of the vision is recorded at the beginning of the account. It is in two forms, in the twenty-fifth year after the exile of Ezekiel who was taken to Babylon with Jehoiachin and other leaders in 597 BCE, and fourteen years after the fall of Jerusalem in 587, that is, 573 BCE.

128

This double dating not only fixes the vision in history, it also specifi-cally relates it to what Ezekiel saw as the two major incidents in God's judgement on exiled Israel. Israel had been deprived of the monarchy with its promise of a continuing line of Davidic kings in the exile of Jehoiachin (on the promise to David, see II Sam.7). In the exile of 587 it had been deprived of the land, the temple and the city of Jerusalem, all things that had come to it by the promise and action of God. What follows in chs.40–48 sets out the recovery of God's promises for the restored people and the way for them to live in those promises.

On the tenth day of the first month of the year 573 BCE, the hand of the Lord took the prophet in 'visions of God' to the city and put him on a very high mountain, opposite the city buildings (vv.1–2). There the prophet met a man whose appearance (*like a figure of bronze*, that is, a brilliant, shining figure) showed him to be a divine messenger (v.3). The man had *a measuring rod* and *a cord* with which to measure the temple complex and provide measurements to be used by the prophet to instruct the people of Israel (v.4).

The outer wall and the east gate
40.5–16

The ground plan of the temple was laid out before the prophet by means of the measurement of its parts, beginning with the outer wall of the temple and the east gate. In the vision the temple area was enclosed by a wall, approximately three metres high, that is, six *long cubits*, with the long cubit being approximately half a metre in length (v.5). The east gate which was the main entrance to the temple area was measured and its main features noted. It was of impressive size and provided with *cells* for temple officials to keep watch over those who entered the temple area (v.6–7). Gates of this kind provided the impressive entrances to temples and cities of the ancient world.

The outer and inner courts
40.17–37

Similar gates were situated in the northern and southern sides of the wall (vv.20–27). These gates led into the outer court which was the place of worship for the people (vv.17–19). There was no gate in the western wall because of the building placed against that wall (see 41.12).

Within the outer wall there was another wall which enclosed the inner court, the court of the priests. The inner wall had gates similar in size and design to those in the outer wall and opposite them (vv.28–37).

Provision for preparation of the offerings
40.38–47

The description of the progress of the prophet and his guide was interrupted to describe the provision for washing and slaughtering *the whole-offering, the purification-offering and the reparation-offering* (vv.38–43). Purification-offerings were made to restore the worshipper to cultic purity and reparation-offerings were fines paid for damage to people or property. The whole-offering was a regular public sacrifice in which, as the name suggests, the whole animal was consumed by fire. It was a sacrifice of thanksgiving. Two rooms were provided at the north and south gates for the priests who had charge of these operations, one for the Zadokite priests and the other for the Levites (vv.44–47; for the distinction between the two orders of priests see 44.6–31).

Measurement of the temple
40.48–41.4

The various parts of the temple itself were measured next. These consisted of a *vestibule* (vv.48–49), the *sanctuary* (41.1–2) and the *inner sanctuary* called the *Holy of Holies* (vv.3–4). Ezekiel, as a priest, was permitted to enter all parts of the temple except the Holy of Holies, so the account makes clear that the man *went into the inner sanctuary* on his own to measure it (v.3).

This bare account of the temple plan has been filled out by a number of detailed passages which aimed to give more information on the temple structure (41.5–42.14). The original account resumes at 42.15.

Details of the temple and its decoration

41.5–26

The temple had a series of terraced arcades or side-chambers on three sides giving a total of 90 rooms; this is similar to the account of Solomon's temple (I Kings 6.5–10) and appears to be based on it. The use to which the rooms were put is not known. A raised platform on which the temple stood extended beyond the walls of the structure to give an open space of 5 cubits round the temple. The platform itself was surrounded by an open space 20 cubits wide (vv.8–11). A building of unspecified use was to the west of the temple (v.12).

41.15b–26 describes the decoration of the temple interior. The vestibule and the two inner rooms of the temple were panelled; that is, the sanctuary and the Holy of Holies. The panelling was carved with *cherubim and palm trees* (vv.18–20). This is similar to the description in I Kings 6.29 and appears to be dependent on it.

The altar that *seemed like an altar of wood in front of the Holy Place*, the Holy of Holies (see I Kings 6.20–22), was the table for the shewbread or bread of the presence. On this table twelve loaves were placed each Sabbath as a food-offering to the Lord and a sign of God's eternal presence with the covenant people (Ex.25.30; Lev.24.5–9).

The priests' rooms

42.1–14

The text of this passage is difficult so that a reconstruction of the text is required before a translation may be attempted (footnotes in REB indicate some of the major points of reconstruction). The passage describes two buildings which were on the northern and southern sides of the building west of the temple. Each appears to have consisted of three parallel blocks, built following the rise in the ground to give a stepped appearance (v.6), but architectural details of these buildings are obscure.

The purpose of the chambers within the buildings was to provide places for the priests to eat their portions of the offerings, a place to store offerings until needed, and a place for the priests to robe and disrobe before and after service at the altar (vv.13–14). They thus provided the means for protecting lay worshippers from contact with the holy and the holy from being defiled by contact with people or things that were profane. This was achieved by the *outside walls* which protected the buildings from the outer court (vv.7,10) and provided the entrances from the outer court (vv.9,12).

The overall measurements
42.15–20

Measurement of the whole area completes the account of the plan for the temple and its courts. The final measurements revealed the total area of the temple complex as a square of 500 cubits. It also made the important point that the outer wall formed the division between the sacred area of the temple and the secular area outside (v.20).

A NOTE ON THE PLAN OF THE TEMPLE IN EZEKIEL 40–48.

The plan of the temple given in this vision account is similar to that found in the descriptions of the temple built by Solomon (I Kings 6–7; II Chron.3) and the tabernacle Moses was instructed to build (Exod.25–31). This suggests that Ezekiel knew the traditions of the tabernacle and its dimensions and/or had access to the dimensions of the temple either by having seen it or through the tradition preserved in I Kings and II Chronicles.

The similarities point to the importance of the temple in Ezekiel's presentation of the reconstruction of Israel. In the account of the formation of Israel as God's covenant people early provision was made for a place for the people to worship God (Exod.25–31). By placing the account of the vision of the temple at the beginning of his plan for the reconstructed Israel, the importance of the temple in the life of the returned exiles was stressed. It also presents the restoration and renewal in terms of the traditions of the beginning of Israel as the people of God.

Further, similarity to the tabernacle and to Solomon's temple provided continuity with the traditions of the covenant and the settlement in Canaan for the returned exiles. Those who returned would know themselves to be heirs to the promises of God to the people Israel. Continuity was important to Ezekiel, as the scheme for the distribution of the tribes in the land in chs.47–48 shows.

The return of the glory of God to the temple
43.1–12

The return of the restored and renewed people and the completion of the temple would supply the necessary conditions for the return of the glory of God to the temple. These conditions would be the opposite of those described in the vision narrative of chs.8–11 when the glory of God departed from the temple.

In the return of the glory of God the temple vision reached its climax for, in this action, God took possession of the temple which was built at God's instigation and for the purpose God would prescribe (v.7a). It was a sign that Israel was restored, for the glory of God had departed as a symbol of judgement, it would return as a symbol of restoration.

The glory of God departed from the east gate (11.23) so it would return by the same gate and from the east (vv.1,2,4; compare with 11.23). The prophet identified the glory of God with what he saw in earlier visions (v.3) when he was called to be a prophet (1.28) and at the destruction of the temple (chs. 10,11). This may be a later addition to the vision account but it is important to the overall message of the book. That is, the God who called the prophet and who was responsible for the judgement, punishment and destruction of Israel was also the God who would restore, renew, and again be among the people of Israel. A spirit transported him to the inner court (v.5; see also 3.12;8.3;11.1) where he *saw the glory of the Lord fill the temple* and heard the voice of God claim the temple as God's throne, footstool and everlasting dwelling place among the Israelites (vv.6,7a). The *throne* and *footstool* take up terms used in relation to the ark to affirm the relationship between the God of Israel and this temple building (throne, Jer.14.21; 17.12; footstool, Pss.99.5; 132.7). The ark itself is not mentioned and does not appear to have survived the exile (see Jer.3.16–17).

43.7–12   A condition for God dwelling *among the Israelites for ever* (v.7a) was that they must not be defile the temple as they had in the past. Two things were banned from the temple – *wanton idolatry* (Hebrew, 'harlotry', which makes the connection with the prominent theme of unfaithfulness in chs. 16 and 23) and the burial of dead kings, or raising their memorials, in the precinct of the temple (vv.7b–9). The latter may refer to burials or memorials in the temple court, or, as the explanation in v.8 suggests, in the grounds of the

133

palace which shared the same area in the old temple/palace complex. Whichever it is, the statement is a clear condemnation of the monarchy and its practices, an element in the later regulations for the 'prince' (45.7–9; 46.18). It also made clear the distinction between the sacred, what was within the outer wall, and the profane, what was outside that wall.

The instruction to tell the people about the temple and to show them the plan recalls the command with which the vision began and so provides a conclusion to this part of the vision (vv.10–11). There is a play on the words 'statutes' and 'laws' (translated *elevation* and *plan*) which suggests that the temple represents for Israel an opportunity for faithfulness and loyalty to God. It also forms a bridge to the cultic legislation which follows.

Regulations for the temple cult
43.13–46.24

The altar of burnt offering
43.13–27

This is the beginning of the ordinances for the temple which extend to ch.46.24, all of which are later than the temple vision account. The measurements of the altar which stood in the inner court (40.47) are given first (vv.13–17). The design of this altar was similar to the ziggurat (a stepped tower) used in Babylonian worship. It is notable that it had steps (v.17) and, although it is not said, was probably made from hewn stones. Both of these features are forbidden in the earlier Book of the Covenant (see Exod.20.24–26); however, there are indications that different types of altars were used in Israel during the period of the monarchy and after the exile (see, for example, I Kings 1.50; 2.28; II Kings 16.10–16; II Chron.4.1). The altar described by Ezekiel may have been patterned on one in use in Jerusalem before the exile and seen by him prior to his removal to Babylon.

Regulations for the consecration of the altar are given in vv.18–27. This involved special sacrifices which were necessary to cleanse the altar of the contamination which adhered to profane objects and to prepare the altar for its holy purpose. These sacrifices were offered for seven days and, at the end of that time, the altar was pronounced

'ritually clean', consecrated and available for use for regular sacrificial practice, by which God would accept the people (v.26–27).
Although this is phrased in the form of regulations it has the introduction and conclusion of an oracle which is intended to tell the
people how they could offer right worship to God.

Closure of the outer east gate
44.1–3

The importance of the east gate as the gate through which the glory
of God entered the temple is emphasised by the decree that it be permanently closed (vv.1–2). No one could use it to gain entry to the
sanctuary (the temple complex). The prince was permitted to eat his
sacrificial meal in the gate building but he was required to enter it
from the outer court (v.3). The special place and requirements for the
prince are given in chs.45.16–17, 21–25; 46.1–12, 16–18 (in relation to
the temple) and 45.7–9; 48.21–22 (his allocation in the distribution of
the land).

Foreigners and levites in the sanctuary
44.4–14

Verses 5–6 of this section are an introduction to the main regulations
for the temple. They stress the importance of what follows by referring to the glory of God in the temple and calling for close attention
to the *rules and regulations of the Lord's house* (vv.4–5).

As a preamble a charge is made against the Israelites that they
allowed foreigners and those *uncircumcised in mind and body* into the
sanctuary and even allowed them to be in charge of the sanctuary.
This gave them charge of *my holy things*, which was an abomination
in God's sight (vv.6–8). Foreigners had been used for menial tasks in
the service of God; for example, Gibeonite slaves were allowed to
'cut wood and draw water ... for the altar of the Lord' (Josh.9.23,27),
and Carites, mercenaries recruited from the Philistines, were
employed as temple guards (II Kings 11.4–19). Such people were
banned from the new temple and its renewed cult.

The charge is made wider when those described as *uncircumcised
in mind* (heart) *and body* (flesh) are included. An uncircumcised heart
was a sign of stubbornness and rebellion among the people of Israel

(Deut.10.16; 30.6; Jer.4.4; 9.26) which suggests that Ezekiel's charge was also against unfaithful Israelites who served in the temple. It may have applied to the levites who were charged with being idolatrous and were demoted to lower orders of service in the temple (vv.9–14). Foreigners would be excluded from the sanctuary and levites would be given the menial tasks the foreigners had performed. Levites would not be permitted to perform any priestly tasks, nor would they have charge of any holy things (vv.13–14).

Regulations for the priests, the Zadokites
44.15–31

The Zadokites, who were judged to have been faithful to God, would be the priests to have charge of the sanctuary, serve God by offering the sacrifices and have the care of the holy things of the sanctuary (vv.15–16). The origin of the Zadokites is obscure. They may have been priests in Jerusalem before David captured the city and remained as priests in the Jerusalem temple through the period of the monarchy. The levites on the other hand may have been displaced priests from the country shrines closed in the reform of Josiah (II Kings 22–23), who were to be given opportunity to act as priests in Jerusalem if they desired to do so (Deut.18.6–8). The record of the reform suggests they did not take up this opportunity because of the jealousy of the Zadokites (II Kings 23.8–9). The Zadokite position would have been strengthened by the charge that the levites had served in the 'high places' of the alien cults. Approval of the Zadokites in vv.15–16 conflicts with Ezekiel's charge against the Jerusalem priests in 8.16, but it may reflect the reality of the situation in the post-exilic period. That is, the Zadokite priests performed all priestly duties and the levites were temple servants.

Regulations for the priests cover the duties in which they would be involved; that is, appropriate dress to protect the people from contact with holy things (vv.17–19), personal matters – length of hair, drinking wine (vv.20–21), restrictions on whom they may marry (v.22), and prohibitions on contact with dead bodies (with exceptions for family members, v.25) and eating carrion (v.31), and provision for mourning purification rites (vv.26–27). Priests would have no inheritance nor possess any land (no land in the tribal allocation, Deut.10.9; 18.2), but they would receive what was devoted to God in the grain, purification and reparation offerings, along with the first fruits and contributions of the people (vv.28–30). They were to give instruction on cultic matters and act to decide certain lawsuits as earlier priests had done (vv.23–24; I Sam.1.9; 4.18; 7.15–17; 9.12–13). Parallel regulations are to be found in the priestly legislation in Leviticus 6,10 and 21, and in Exodus and Numbers.

Allocation of the land – the sacred reserve
   45.1–8

Requirements for allocation of the land by tribe among the returning exiles are given in 47.13–48.29. The land was to be divided from north to south into horizontal strips with each tribe being allocated a portion. At the centre of the land a further strip was to be set apart for the temple, priests and levites, the city and the prince (48.8–22). 45.1–8 deals specifically with the allocation of this central portion of land within the context of regulations for the temple. A *sacred reserve*, 25,000 cubits square, would occupy the central portion of the special strip (v.1) and have on either side of it the allocation to the *ruler* (prince, v.7). The square would be divided into three horizontal strips, two 10,000 cubits wide and one 5,000 cubits wide. The central strip (10,000 cubits) would be for the priests and would have within it a plot 500 cubits square for the sanctuary, 'the holiest place of all'. The northern strip (10,000 cubits) would be for the levites and the southern strip (5,000 cubits) for the city. The city strip would be a common possession, it would belong to 'all Israel' (v.6).

This regulation makes two important points for restored Israel. First, the temple would be at the centre of the life of the renewed Israel, a point made in the regulations for the temple in chs.44–46 and now emphasised by the requirement to place the temple at the geographical centre of the nation. Second, the sacredness of the sanctuary/temple is emphasised by being set within the priests' allocation of land, not within the city, so that it would be protected from contact with things that were profane such as the city and the life of its people.

The *ruler* (prince) would have the remainder of the strip as *his share in Israel* (v.8). The critical comment on the rulers in v.8b is an addition to lead in to the regulations for rulers which follow. It suggests that, with a generous land allocation of their own, rulers would not be tempted to take land which was given to the people (see 46.16–17).

Regulations for the rulers
45.9–17

These regulations begin with a call to the rulers to uphold justice in their dealings with the people (v.9) which was made against a background of experience of rulers (kings) of the past, referred to in 22.6; 34.1–10, and portrayed in the action of King Ahab in taking the land of Naboth (I Kings 21.1–16). It is important to note that the title used for the secular ruler in these regulations is 'prince' (Hebrew, *nasi*, translated 'ruler' in REB) and not 'king' (Hebrew, *melek*), the term used during the period of the monarchy. This change of title indicates a change in the role of the secular leader. As the regulations that follow show, the major tasks relate to upholding justice and providing for the cultic life of the people. Indeed, it may be that we should see the whole of 45.9 to 46.18 as dealing mainly with the ruler(s), with 45.9 as the introduction and 46.18 the conclusion.

Justice was to be observed in the measures and weights used to determine the offerings the people were to bring to the temple. A *homer* was the standard measure by volume, with the *ephah* a dry measure, one tenth of a *homer*, and the *bath* a liquid measure, one tenth of a *homer*. The *shekel* was the standard for weight and was equal to 20 *gerah* and one fiftieth of a *mina* (vv.10–12). Verse 9 suggests the ruler would be responsible for maintaining these standards.

The contributions set out in vv.13–15 form a temple tax to provide for the sacrifices and the temple personnel. The ruler would receive these contributions and be responsible for the sacrifices for the expiation of the people (vv.16–17).

Regulations for purification of the temple and for major festivals
45.18–25

Regulations for the purification of the sanctuary (vv.18–20) are similar to those for the purification of the altar (43.18–27). In the case of the temple the requirement is for an annual ceremony which would include sacrifice and smearing blood on parts of the temple, altar and inner court (vv.18–19). The instruction to *do the same on the seventh day of the month* (v.20) suggests that the cleansing concluded on the seventh day (similarly Lev.23.8). The addition *the man who has sinned through inadvertence or ignorance* appears to be taking up the requirements for purification for such sin found in Lev.4.13 and Num.15.22 to explain why regular purification of the temple would be necessary.

45.21–25 The Passover and Ingathering festivals are provided for here with the major interest in giving regulations for the role of the ruler and the purification of the community. Passover celebrated the release of the people of Israel from slavery in Egypt and God's 'passing over' the Israelite homes when the eldest child of the Egyptians was killed (Exod.12.1–13). Originally the festival was celebrated in the family home (Exod.12.1–2) but, with Deuteronomy (16.1–2), it became an annual pilgrimage festival for all adult males. Here it is joined to the feast of Unleavened Bread (as in Deut.16.1–8), a period of seven days in which only bread without yeast could be eaten (Exod.23.15). During the celebration of the festival the ruler would supply the animals required for the sacrifices. The Passover is here understood as an opportunity for a purification offering (vv.22,23).

The ruler would also supply the offerings necessary for the feast of Ingathering (v.25: REB *pilgrim-feast*). This was originally an agricultural festival which was later associated with the Israel's wilderness experience of dwelling in tents (Lev.23.33–43; Deut.16.13). These regulations make it another opportunity for a purification-offering (v.25).

Worship and further duties of the ruler
46.1–18

The outer east gate would be permanently closed (44.1–3) and the inner east gate would be closed on all days except the sabbath and at new moon. On the sabbath the ruler would be allowed to enter the inner east gate from the outer court and proceed to the door to the inner court. From there he would watch his sacrifices being made and offer his worship. The people could bow at the entrance to the gate on sabbaths and at new moon, but they could not enter the gate (vv.2–3).

46.4–7 lay down the provisions to be made by the ruler for sabbath and new moon sacrifices. These consist of animal, grain and oil offerings. The requirements are greater than those listed in the priestly regulations in Num.28.9–15. There is no satisfactory explanation for these differences but that should not be allowed to divert our attention from the important role of the ruler in providing the offerings for sabbath and new moon celebrations.

46.8–10   regulate the movement of the ruler and people within the sanctuary. This may be an exercise in crowd control, but it also clears up any misunderstanding about the ruler and the inner east gate. The prince could not enter the inner court so he would enter the gate from the outer court and, after he had completed his worship, would be required to go out by the same way (v.8). On festal days, when there would be large numbers of worshippers, the people would enter the outer court by one gate and go out by the opposite gate (v.9). The statement that the ruler would *be among them, going in when they go in and coming out when they come out*, following closely on v.9, suggests a procession at the head of which would be the ruler. This would be a further indication of the importance of his cultic role.

46.11 is an addition to these regulations on the ruler and provision for worship in the temple. It appears to be a correction to 45.24 which omitted the requirement of a lamb from the offerings.

The ruler's position is recognised further in the regulation that the inner east gate would be opened for him to make a voluntary offering (v.12).

46.13–15   set out regulations for daily offerings of a lamb and grain-offering. They would be offered every morning, which differs from the priestly requirement in which two yearling rams were to be offered, one in the morning and one in the evening, along with grain-offerings (Num.28.3–8). It appears to be a general requirement (*you must provide ...*) included here to give an overall coverage of the sacrificial system. However, by its inclusion in this body of material on the ruler (45.9–46.18), there is the suggestion that the ruler would be responsible for provision of the daily offerings, as well as those specified in the other regulations.

46.16–17   lay down restrictions on the way in which the ruler used his land. He could give land to his sons and it would have to remain in his family, but no other gifts of a permanent nature could be made. If the ruler gave land to a slave, that gift would last only until the Jubilee Year when the slave would be released and the land would revert to its owner (Lev.25.8–17)

46.18   The final word on the ruler (except for the land distribution in 48.21–22) forbade him from taking the land that belonged to the people. Their land belonged to their families and could not be taken by another, not even the ruler. His provision of land would be sufficient for him and his family.

From this treatment of the ruler we see three things:

1. He would have honoured status, as his place for worship in the temple shows.

2. He would have an important role in the functioning of the cult. He would not be a priest, therefore he could not offer sacrifice, but he would have responsibility to ensure provision was made for the sacrifices required in the temple cult.

3. He would have an area of land set aside for him and his family. This would give him independence as it would support him without the need for taxes, but it would also put limits on him. He could not dispose of his land, nor could he take the land of the people. In this the ruler would be different from the pre-exilic king, and deliberately so. His task would be to serve the temple and uphold *what is right and just* (45.9).

The temple kitchens
   46.19–24

The description of the places for preparation of food for the priests (vv.19–20) and the people (vv.21–24) is a supplement to the report on the priest's rooms given in 42.1–14 and emphasises the division between the priests (v.20) and the *attendants* (levites, v.24). Priests would deal with what was holy, which could not be allowed to contact the profane and thereby be contaminated. Nor could holiness be permitted to be transmitted to the people, for that would endanger them. So separate provision was made for the preparation of food for the priests and for the people.

The river of life and allocation of the land
47–48

The life-giving river
47.1–12

The account of the life-giving river continues the temple vision and brings it to its conclusion. The vision account had been interrupted by the inclusion of regulations for the temple (44.3–46.24). In this conclusion to the vision the prophet saw a stream which began at the eastern entrance to the temple and flowed east to the Dead Sea, increasing in size as it flowed so that it watered the desert and, when it reached the Dead Sea, its great volume of water made the salt water fresh. So it would give life to what was dead.

The original account has been added to by those who desired to emphasise the importance of the temple and to show how it would transform the life of Israel (vv.7,9–11). Trees would grow on the river's banks, living creatures would draw life from it and the Dead Sea would produce an abundance of fish. So the temple would bring new life to Israel as the spirit brought new life to the bones in the vision of the valley of dry bones (ch.37). A practical comment provides for salt-pans to be preserved to meet the need for salt which was necessary for the preservation of food and for use in the cult (v.11).

Accounts of a river by which God would bring blessings on the people are strong in the traditions of Israel. The creation account of the second chapter of Genesis tells of a river flowing from Eden which not only watered the garden, but was also the source of four great rivers that watered the earth. Psalm 46.4 tells of 'a river whose streams bring joy to the city of God, the holy dwelling of the Most High'. Ezekiel has taken this tradition and used it to express the conviction that the people restored from exile by God would have in the temple an assurance of God's presence with them, for it would provide them with the means to respond to God through the celebration of the properly ordered cult, and thus maintain their relationship with God, and it would be the source of blessing by which God would sustain them in the transformed land, expressed in rich symbolism in the vision of the river. Ezekiel had in mind a restored people in a renewed land which was pictured as a new Eden, a tradition taken up also in the prophetic works of Joel (3.18) and Zechariah (13.1;14.8), and in the New Testament (Rev.22.1–2).

Allocation of the land
  47.13–48.29

There is an abrupt change from the vision account of vv.1–12 to regulations for the allocation of the land in 47.13–48.29. This is introduced with the messenger formula, *The Lord God says*, and the instruction to divide the land equally among the twelve tribes, for what they received would be their inheritance (vv.13–14). The allocation of two portions to Joseph to be given to Manasseh and Ephraim, sons of Joseph, maintains the number of tribal portions at twelve and compensates for Levi having a special allocation in the sacred area. The presentation of the allocation is in four parts: 47.13–23, the boundaries of the land; 48.1–7, the tribes to the north; 48.8–22, the central strip; 48.23–29, the tribes to the south.

The borders of the land and provision for foreigners (47.13–23)

The boundaries for the land are clearly ideal and very similar to the priestly legislation in Numbers 34.1–12. The most obvious difference between them is that for Ezekiel the eastern boundary would be the Jordan river while the priestly account included an area to the east of the Jordan where two and a half tribes were to be settled (the Reubenites, Gadites and half the tribe of Manasseh, Num.34.13–15). Eastern and western boundaries would be the clear geographical features of the Jordan to the east and the Great Sea (Mediterranean) to the west, but the location of the northern and southern boundaries is uncertain. The northern border would extend to Lebo-hamath (v.15), but the location of that place is not known. Ezek.6.14 suggests the border was near Riblah, which was to the north of Damascus. To the south the boundary would be an arc extending from the Dead Sea to Tamar, Kadesh-barnea (associated with the 'waters of Meribah' [strife], Num.20.2–13) and the Great Sea, via the 'Brook of Egypt' (v.19; see Josh.15.4; I Kings 8.65). The boundaries envisaged would be similar to those of the kingdoms of David and Solomon (I Kings 8.65).

47.21–23   The command to distribute the land among the tribes is stated in v.21 but description of the distribution is delayed by a command to include resident *aliens* (foreigners) in the distribution, for they would have a share of land in whatever tribe they may have been resident (vv.21–23). *Aliens* living in Israel prior to the exile were not permitted to own land but they were protected by the law (Exod.22.21; 23.9; Deut.14.29; 24.14–15, 17–22). Later law codes say they were to be treated as *native Israelites* (Lev.19.34; 24.22; Num.15.29), but it is only here that it is suggested that resident aliens who, presumably, had accepted the faith of Israel, should be included in any land allocation (compare with Isa.56.1–8).

Allocation to the tribes to the north of the sacred area (48.1–7)

The land would be divided into parallel strips across its full width from east to west and allocated in listed order from north to south. This allocation is different from that found in Josh.13–19, a difference which appears to have resulted from four factors. First, the tribes previously situated to the east of the Jordan had to be fitted into the new national borders. Second, the sacred reserve is a new feature in the allocation which required a change to allow it space in the identified land area (47.13–19). Third, the sacred reserve influenced the position of the tribes in relation to itself. The sons of Jacob's wives would be nearest to the sacred reserve; that is, Judah, Reuben, Ephraim and Manasseh to the north and Benjamin, Simeon, Issachar and Zebulun to the south. The sons from Jacob's concubines would receive allocations at the extremities of the land; that is, Dan, Asher and Naphtali to the north, and Gad in the south. Fourth, in order to have the sacred reserve in the middle of the land, some tribes previously to the north of Jerusalem would be placed in the south, that is, Benjamin, Issachar and Zebulun. The final scheme was for seven tribes north of the sacred area and five tribes south of it.

The sacred reserve (48.8–22)

Provision for *the sacred reserve* and an allocation of land for the prince was discussed in comments on 45.1–8. In this longer version further details and some additions have been included. The whole area would be sacred and therefore could not be alienated in any way (v.20). This is made clear in v.14 which forbids sale or exchange because the area *is holy to the Lord*.

Details of the area for the city are also given (vv.15–19). It would be in the centre of its allotment with common land and areas to the east and west for the production of food.

48.11–12   An addition here makes it clear that the priests referred to in vv.9–10 would be the Zadokite priests. It is a polemical comment on the relative status of the Zadokites and the levites. The Zadokites would preserve the holiness of the temple and protect the people from that holiness as they served in the temple and dealt with the holy things of the cult while the levites performed the menial tasks associated with the temple (44.9–19). Preservation of the holiness of the temple by this regulation included placing the temple in the middle of the land of the priests, the Zadokites, for their area *will be most sacred* (v.12).

Allocation to tribes south of the sacred area (48.23–29)

The scheme for allocation of land to the south of the sacred area is the same as that for the north.

The city
48.30–35

A concluding postscript has been added to the account of the temple vision (chs.40–48). It gives the measurements of the city's boundaries (as in v.16) and the names of the gates leading out of the city. There would be three gates on each of the four sides of the city, each named after one of the tribes. It is notable that Joseph and Levi are named instead of Manasseh and Ephraim, although they are not among the tribes allocated land in the scheme set out in vv.1–7, 23–27. This suggests these verses are from another tradition, harking back to the earlier tradition of Israel as given in Jacob's blessing of his sons (Gen.49.2–27) and aiming to maintain continuity with the Israel which received God's promises in the past.

48.35   The final verse gives the circumference measurement of the city and states that the city would be named *The Lord is there*, a sign that it would be renewed and that God would be with the people. The new temple and the renewed city would be the people's assurance that God was with them and the basis for their continued hope and trust in God.

WORSHIP AND RESPONSE TO GOD

This part of the book of Ezekiel completes the statement of Israel's understanding of its relationship with God in the light of its experience prior to exile, in exile and as a people returned from exile. Its purpose is to assert that God would dwell in the midst of the restored and renewed people and that they would find their fulfilment through their response in service to God. For Ezekiel the main focus of this response was to worship God in the temple. There the people would be aware of the presence of God whose glory would return to the temple and who would receive the sacrifices offered in observance of the cult requirements.

To emphasise the centrality of the temple in the life of the restored people the author presented a ground plan of the temple and the requirements for its rebuilding. Provisions for the cult and its ordering are given also. Even the role of the 'secular' leader, the 'prince', is described in terms of his relation to the temple and its cult, while the directions for the division of the land among the tribes specify that the temple would have its own special area which would be (almost) central among the tribes. Above all, the *glory of the God of Israel* (43.2) would return to the rebuilt temple, assuring the people of God's presence in their place of worship and in their midst.

The whole presentation emphasises response through the service of the cult as provided in the temple.

The particular form of worship response Ezekiel proposed reflects the emphasis in other places in the book where he condemns the people for their cultic sins. Ezekiel condemned the people for their corrupt society and called for repentance and observance of laws which are close to those formulated in the Ten Commandments (ch.18), but his fiercest condemnation was pronounced against cultic sins and the defiling of the temple (see especially chs. 8–11). When offering the people grounds for hope, the prophet looked to the eradication of alien cult elements, the provision of acceptable practices and the location of a *sanctuary in their midst for all time* (37.26). So, when provision was made for the restored and renewed society, the major emphasis was on the correct response to God in cult and worship. This was a primary means by which the people would express their loyalty to God.

This form of cultic emphasis may derive quite naturally from the influence of the prophet, whose priestly origin is referred to in 1.3, and his circle of followers. However, we need to acknowledge that, when considering how people may respond to God, some form of worship will be part of that response. What Ezekiel says is that it should have a high priority and be in a form that would be acceptable to God. It is an integral part of relationship with God.

Christians acknowledge worship as an essential part of our relationship with God. The church throughout its history has maintained the centrality of worship and provided for it in many forms while focusing on response to what God has done and the assurance of God's leading into the future. Put simply, worship is a necessary part of the Christian life. It is part of our heritage as people of God and, as such, it speaks to us and to the world at large of our identity as people of God, an identity which is derived from acknowledgment of what God has done and is doing in the world, and from the response we make to God in praise and thanksgiving.

Present-day Christians carry on the traditions of worship found in the New Testament and the life of the early church in which the eucharist and the proclamation of Christ, the Word of God, are central. They provide the focus for worship which may take various forms depending on the emphases of that part of the Christian heritage to which we belong and the demands of the culture and community in which we are set.

The traditions of the faith and the need of the present, are the focal points of worship and the means of our being able to offer worship that is response to God. Our worship is a celebration of the presence of God among us; remembering, in the sense of making present to us, the great acts of God for all humankind, and doing it in terms of the life we are now living. That is, such worship is a present experience which appropriates the past and brings us into the reality of our relationship with God in Jesus Christ. Ezekiel pointed to a response which, through the practice of the cult, recalled the great acts of God known from the past and the promises made to the exiles. This response was to be made in the context of life lived as the returned and restored people of God. That the provisions of chs.40-48 do not appear to have been realised is beside the point. Ezekiel points to the need for this response as part of the continuing life of the people of God.

What Ezekiel did for the people who had returned from exile to live in their own land we are called to do as an ongoing task; to provide for ourselves and all who share community with us opportunity to celebrate the grace of God to us as it is seen in Jesus Christ, in our lives and in the lives of those who have gone before us, and to acknowledge our place within the relationship with God.